Why God Became Man

Cur Deus Homo

Why God Became Man

Cur Deus Homo

St. Anselm of Canterbury

TAN Books
Gastonia, North Carolina

This edition of *Why God Became Man – Cur Deus Homo* is from the edition published by The Open Court Publishing Company, Chicago, 1926. It was retypeset and published in 2025 by TAN Books.

Cover design by Caroline Green

ISBN: 978-1-5051-3610-4
Kindle ISBN: 978-1-5051-3746-0
ePUB ISBN: 978-1-5051-3745-3

Published in the United States by
TAN Books
PO Box 269
Gastonia, NC 28053
www.TANBooks.com

Printed in the United States of America

Contents

Preface

The first part of this book was copied without my knowledge, before the work had been completed and revised. I have therefore been obliged to finish it as best I could, more hurriedly, and so more briefly, than I wished. For had an undisturbed and adequate period been allowed me for publishing it, I should have introduced and subjoined many things about which I have been silent. For it was while suffering under great anguish of heart, the origin and reason of which are known to God, that, at the entreaty of others, I began the book in England, and finished it when an exile in Capra. From the theme on which it was published I have called it *Cur Deus Homo*, and have divided it into two short books. The first contains the objections of infidels, who despise the Christian faith because they deem it contrary to reason; and also the reply of believers; and, in fine, leaving Christ out of view (as if nothing had ever been known of him), it proves, by absolute reasons, the impossibility that any man should be saved without him. Again, in the second book, likewise, as if nothing were known of Christ, it is moreover shown by plain reasoning and fact that human nature was ordained for this purpose, viz., that every man should enjoy a happy immortality, both in body and in soul; and that it was necessary that this design for which man was made should be fulfilled; but that it could not be fulfilled unless God became man, and unless all things were to take place which we hold with regard to Christ. I request all who may wish to copy this book to prefix this brief preface, with the heads of the whole work, at its commencement; so that, into whosesoever hands it may fall, as he looks on the face of it, there may be nothing in the whole body of the work which shall escape his notice.

Book First

CHAPTER I

The question on which the whole work rests.

I have been often and most earnestly requested by many, both personally and by letter, that I would hand down in writing the proofs of a certain doctrine of our faith, which I am accustomed to give to inquirers; for they say that these proofs gratify them, and are considered sufficient. This they ask, not for the sake of attaining to faith by means of reason, but that they may be gladdened by understanding and meditating on those things which they believe; and that, as far as possible, they may be always ready to convince any one who demands of them a reason of that hope which is in us. And this question, both infidels are accustomed to bring up against us, ridiculing Christian simplicity as absurd; and many believers ponder it in their hearts; for what cause or necessity, in sooth, God became man, and by his own death, as we believe and affirm, restored life to the world; when he might have done this, by means of some other being, angelic or human, or merely by his will. Not only the learned, but also many unlearned persons interest themselves in this inquiry and seek for its solution. Therefore, since many desire to consider this subject, and, though it seem very difficult in the investigation, it is yet plain to all in the solution, and attractive for the value and beauty of the reasoning; although what ought to be sufficient has been said by the holy fathers and their successors, yet I will take pains to disclose to inquirers what God has seen fit to lay open to me. And since investigations, which are carried on by question and answer, are thus made more plain to many, and especially to less quick minds, and on that account are more gratifying, I will take to argue with me one of those persons who agitate this subject; one, who among the rest impels me more earnestly to it, so that in this way Boso may question and Anselm reply.

Chapter II

How those things which are to be said should be received.

Boso. As the right order requires us to believe the deep things of Christian faith before we undertake to discuss them by reason; so to my mind it appears a neglect if, after we are established in the faith, we do not seek to understand what we believe. Therefore, since I thus consider myself to hold the faith of our redemption, by the prevenient grace of God, so that, even were I unable in any way to understand what I believe, still nothing could shake my constancy; I desire that you should discover to me, what, as you know, many besides myself ask, for what necessity and cause God, who is omnipotent, should have assumed the littleness and weakness of human nature for the sake of its renewal?

Anselm. You ask of me a thing which is above me, and therefore I tremble to take in hand subjects too lofty for me, lest, when some one may have thought or even seen that I do not satisfy him, he will rather believe that

I am in error with regard to the substance of the truth, than that my intellect is not able to grasp it.

Boso. You ought not so much to fear this, because you should call to mind, on the other hand, that it often happens in the discussion of some question that God opens what before lay concealed; and that you should hope for the grace of God, because if you liberally impart those things which you have freely received, you will be worthy to receive higher things to which you have not yet attained.

Anselm. There is also another thing on account of which I think this subject can hardly, or not at all, be discussed between us comprehensively; since, for this purpose, there is required a knowledge of Power and Necessity and Will and certain other subjects which are so related to one another that none of them can be fully examined without the rest; and so the discussion of these topics requires a separate labor, which, though not very easy, in my opinion, is by no means useless; for ignorance of these subjects makes certain things difficult, which by acquaintance with them become easy.

Boso. You can speak so briefly with regard to these things, each in its place, that we may both have all that is requisite for the present object, and what remains to be said we can put off to another time.

Anselm. This also much disinclines me from your request, not only that the subject is important, but as it is of a form fair above the sons of men, so is it of a wisdom fair above the intellect of men. On this account, I fear, lest, as I am wont to be incensed against sorry artists, when I see our Lord himself painted in an unseemly figure; so also it may fall out with me if I should undertake to exhibit so rich a theme in rough and vulgar diction.

Boso. Even this ought not to deter you, because, as you allow any one to talk better if he can, so you preclude none from writing more elegantly if your language does not please him. But, to cut you off from all excuses, you are not to fulfil this request of mine for the learned but for me, and those asking the same thing with me.

Anselm. Since I observe your earnestness and that of those who desire this thing with you, out of love and pious zeal, I will try to the best of my ability with the assistance of God and your prayers, which, when making this request, you have often promised me, not so much to make plain what you inquire about, as to inquire with you. But I wish all that I say to be received with this understanding, that, if I shall have said anything which higher authority does not corroborate, though I appear to demonstrate it by argument, yet it is not to be received with any further confidence, than as so appearing to me for the time, until God in some way make a clearer revelation to me. But if I am in any measure able to set your inquiry at rest, it should be concluded that a wiser than I will be able to do this more fully; nay, we must understand that for all that a man can say or know still deeper grounds of so great a truth lie concealed.

Boso. Suffer me, therefore, to make use of the words of infidels; for it is proper for us when we seek to investigate the reasonableness of our faith to propose the objections of those who are wholly unwilling to submit to the same faith, without the support of reason. For although they appeal to reason because they do not believe, but we, on the other hand, because we do believe; nevertheless, the thing sought is one and the same. And if you bring up anything in reply which sacred authority seems to oppose, let it be mine to urge this inconsistency until you disprove it.

Anselm. Speak on according to your pleasure.

Chapter III

Objections of infidels and replies of believers.

Boso. Infidels ridiculing our simplicity charge upon us that we do injustice and dishonor to God when we affirm that he descended into the womb of a virgin, that he was born of woman, that he grew on the nourishment of milk and the food of men; and, passing over many other things which seem incompatible with Deity, that he endured fatigue, hunger, thirst, stripes and crucifixion among thieves.

Anselm. We do no injustice or dishonor to God, but give him thanks with all the heart, praising and proclaiming the ineffable height of his compassion. For the more astonishing a thing it is and beyond expectation, that he has restored us from so great and deserved ills in which we were, to so great and unmerited blessings which we had forfeited; by so much the more has he shown his more exceeding love and tenderness towards us. For did they but carefully consider bow fitly in this way human redemption is secured, they would not ridicule our simplicity, but would rather join with us in praising the wise beneficence of God. For, as death came upon the human race by the disobedience of man, it was fitting that by man's obedience life should be restored. And, as sin, the cause of our condemnation, had its origin from a woman, so ought the author of our righteousness and salvation to be born of a woman. And so also was it proper that the devil, who, being man's tempter, had conquered him in eating of the tree, should be vanquished by man in the suffering of the tree which man bore. Many other things also, if we carefully examine them, give a certain indescribable beauty to our redemption as thus procured.

Chapter IV

How these things appear not decisive to infidels, and merely like so many pictures.

Boso. These things must be admitted to be beautiful, and like so many pictures; but, if they have no solid foundation, they do not appear sufficient to infidels, as reasons why we ought to believe that God wished to suffer the things which we speak of. For when one wishes to make a picture, he selects something substantial to paint it upon, so that his picture may remain. For no one paints in water or in air, because no traces of the picture remain in them. Wherefore, when we hold up to infidels these harmonious proportions which you speak of as so many pictures of the real thing, since they do not think this belief of ours a reality, but only a fiction, they consider us, as it were, to be painting upon a cloud. Therefore the rational existence of the truth first be shown, I mean, the necessity, which proves that God ought to or could have condescended to those things which we affirm. Afterwards, to make the body of the truth, so to speak, shine forth more clearly, these harmonious proportions, like pictures of the body, must be described.

Anselm. Does not the reason why God ought to do the things we speak of seem absolute enough when we consider that the human race, that work of his so very precious, was wholly ruined, and that it was not seemly that the purpose which God had made concerning man should fall to the ground; and, moreover, that this purpose could not be carried into effect unless the human race were delivered by their Creator himself?

CHAPTER V

How the redemption of man could not be effected by any other being but God.

Boso. If this deliverance were said to be effected somehow by any other being than God (whether it were an angelic or a human being), the mind of man would receive it far more patiently. For God could have made some man without sin, not of a sinful substance, and not a descendant of any man, but just as he made Adam, and by this man it should seem that the work we speak of could have been done.

Anselm. Do you not perceive that, if any other being should rescue man from eternal death, man would rightly be adjudged as the servant of that being? Now if this be so, he would in no wise be restored to that dignity which would have been his had he never sinned. For he, who was to be through eternity only the servant of God and an equal with the holy angels, would now be the servant of a being who was not God, and whom the angels did not serve.

Chapter VI

How infidels find fault with us for saying that God has redeemed us by his death, and thus has shown his love towards us, and that he came to overcome the devil for us.

Boso. This they greatly wonder at, because we call this redemption a release. For, say they, in what custody or imprisonment, or under whose power were you held, that God could not free you from it, without purchasing your redemption by so many sufferings, and finally by his own blood? And when we tell them that he freed us from our sins, and from his own wrath, and from hell, and from the power of the devil, whom he came to vanquish for us, because we were unable to do it, and that he purchased for us the kingdom of heaven; and that, by doing all these things, he manifested the greatness of his love towards us; they answer: If you say that God, who, as you believe, created the universe by a word, could not do all these things by a simple command, you contradict yourselves, for you make him powerless. Or, if you grant that he could have done these things in some other way, but did not wish to, how can you vindicate his wisdom, when you assert that he desired, without any reason, to suffer things so unbecoming? For these things which you bring up are all regulated by his will; for the wrath of God is nothing but his desire to punish. If, then, he does not desire to punish the sins of men, man is free from his sins, and from the wrath of God, and from hell, and from the power of the devil, all which things are the sufferings of sin; and, what he had lost by reason of these sins, he now regains. For, in whose power is hell, or the devil? Or, whose is the kingdom of heaven, if it be not his who created all things? Whatever things, therefore, you dread or hope for, all lie subject to his will, whom nothing can oppose. If, then, God were unwilling to save the human race in any other way than that you mention, when he could have done it by his simple will, observe, to say the least, how you disparage his wisdom. For, if a man without motive should do, by severe toil, a thing which he could have done in some easy way, no one would consider him a wise man. As to your statement that God has shown in this way how much he loved you, there is no argument to support this, unless it be proved that he could not otherwise have saved man. For, if he could not have done it otherwise, then it was, indeed, necessary for him to manifest his love in this way. But now, when he could have saved man differently, why is it that, for the sake of displaying his love, he does and suffers the things which you enumerate? For does he not show good angels how much he loves them, though he suffer no such things as these for them? As to what you say of his coming to vanquish the devil for you, with what meaning dare you allege this? Is not the omnipotence of God everywhere enthroned? How is it, then, that God must needs come down from heaven to vanquish the devil? These are the objections with which infidels think they can withstand us.

Chapter VII

How the devil had no justice on his side against man; and why it was, that he seemed to have had it, and why God could have freed man in this way.

Moreover, I do not see the force of that argument, which we are wont to make use of, that God, in order to save men, was bound, as it were, to try a contest with the devil in justice, before he did in strength, so that, when the devil should put to death that being in whom there was nothing worthy of death, and who was God, he should justly lose his power over sinners; and that, if it were not so, God would have used undue force against the devil, since the devil had a rightful ownership of man, for the devil had not seized man with violence, but man had freely surrendered to him. It is true that this might well enough be said, if the devil or man belonged to any other being than God, or were in the power of any but God. But since neither the devil nor man belong to any but God, and neither can exist without the exertion of Divine power, what cause ought God to try with his own creature (*de suo, in suo*), or what should he do but punish his servant, who had seduced his fellow-servant to desert their common Lord and come over to himself; who, a traitor, had taken to himself a fugitive; a thief, had taken to himself a fellow-thief, with what he had stolen from his Lord. For when one was stolen from his Lord by the persuasions of the other, both were thieves. For what could be more just than for God to do this? Or, should God, the judge of all, snatch man, thus held, out of the power of him who holds him so unrighteously, either for the purpose of punishing him in some other way than by means of the devil, or of sparing him, what injustice would there be in this? For, though man deserved to be tormented by the devil, yet the devil tormented him unjustly. For man merited punishment, and there was no more suitable way for him to be punished than by that being to whom he had given his consent to sin. But the infliction of punishment was nothing meritorious in the devil; on the other hand, he was even more unrighteous in this, because he was not led to it by a love of justice, but urged on by a malicious impulse. For he did not do this at the command of God, but God's inconceivable wisdom, which happily controls even wickedness, permitted it. And, in my opinion, those who think that the devil has any right in holding man, are brought to this belief by seeing that man is justly exposed to the tormenting of the devil, and that God in justice permits this; and therefore they suppose that the devil rightly inflicts it. For the very same thing, from opposite points of view, is sometimes both just unjust, and hence, by those who do not carefully inspect the matter, is deemed wholly just or wholly unjust. Suppose, for example, that one strikes an innocent person unjustly, and hence justly deserves to beaten himself; if, however, the one who was beaten, though he ought not to avenge himself, yet does strike the person who beat him, then he does it unjustly. And hence this violence on the part of the man who returns the blow is unjust, because he ought not to avenge himself; but as far as he who received the blow is concerned, it is just, for since he gave a blow unjustly, he justly deserves to receive one in return. Therefore, from opposite views, the same action is both just and unjust, for it may chance that one person shall consider it only just, and another only unjust. So also the devil is said to torment men justly, because God in justice permits this, and man in justice suffers it. But when man is said to suffer justly, it is not meant that his just suffering is inflicted by the hand of justice itself, but that he is punished by the just judgment of God. But if that written decree is brought up, which the Apostle says was made against us, and cancelled by the death of Christ; and if any one thinks that it was intended by this decree that the devil, as if under the writing of a sort of compact, should justly demand sin and the punishment of sin, of man, before Christ suffered, as a debt for the first sin to which he tempted man, so that in this way he seems to prove his right over man, I do not by any means think that it is to be so understood. For that writing is not of the devil, because it is called the writing of a decree of the devil, but of God. For by the just judgment of God it was decreed, and, as it were, confirmed by writing, that, since man had sinned, he should not henceforth of himself have the power to avoid sin or the punishment of sin; for the spirit is out-going and not returning (*est enim spiritus vadens et non rediens*); and he who sins ought not to escape with impunity, unless pity spare the sinner, and deliver and restore him. Wherefore we ought not to believe that, on account of this writing, there can be found any justice on the part of the devil in his tormenting man. In fine, as there is never any injustice in a good angel, so in an evil angel there can be no justice at all. There was no reason, therefore, as respects the devil, why God should not make use of as own power against him for the liberation of man.

Chapter VIII

How, although the acts of Christ's condescension which we speak of do not belong to his divinity, it yet seems improper to infidels that these things should be said of him even as a man; and why it appears to them that this man did not suffer death of his own will.

Anselm. The will of God ought to be a sufficient reason for us, when he does anything, though we cannot see why he does it. For the will of God is never irrational.

Boso. That is very true, if it be granted that God does wish the thing in question; but many will never allow that God does wish anything if it be inconsistent with reason.

Anselm. What do you find inconsistent with reason, in our confessing that God desired those things which make up our belief with regard to his incarnation?

Boso. This in brief: that the Most High should stoop to things so lowly, that the Almighty should do a thing with such toil.

Anselm. They who speak thus do not understand our belief. For we affirm that the Divine nature is beyond doubt impassible, and that God cannot at all be brought down from his exaltation, nor *toil* in anything which he wishes to effect. But we say that the Lord Jesus Christ is very God and very man, one person in two natures, and two natures in one person. When, therefore, we speak of God as enduring any humiliation or infirmity, we do not refer to the majesty of that nature, which cannot suffer; but to the feebleness of the human constitution which he assumed. And so there remains no ground of objection against our faith. For in this way we intend no debasement of the Divine nature, but we teach that one person is both Divine and human. In the incarnation of God there is no lowering of the Deity; but the nature of man we believe to be exalted.

Boso. Be it so; let nothing be referred to the Divine nature, which is spoken of Christ after the manner of human weakness; but how will it ever be made out a just or reasonable thing that God should treat or suffer to be treated in such a manner, that man whom the Father called his beloved Son in whom he was well pleased, and whom the Son made himself? For what justice is there in *his* suffering death for the sinner, who was the most just of all men? What man, if he condemned the innocent to free the guilty, would not himself be judged worthy of condemnation? And so the matter seems to return to the same incongruity which is mentioned above. For if he could not save sinners in any other way than by condemning the just, where is his omnipotence? If, however, he could, but did not wish to, how shall we sustain his wisdom and justice?

Anselm. God the Father did not treat that man as you seem to suppose, nor put to death the innocent for the guilty. For the Father did not compel him to suffer death, or even allow him to be slain, against his will, but of his own accord he endured death for the salvation of men.

Boso. Though it were not against his will, since he agreed to the will of the Father; yet the Father seems to have bound him, as it were, by his injunction. For it is said that Christ "humbled himself, being made obedient to the Father even unto death, and that the death of the cross. For which cause God also hath highly exalted him;" and that "he learned obedience from the things which he suffered;" and that God spared not his own Son, but gave him up for us all." And likewise the Son says: "I came not to do my own will, but the will of him that sent me." And when about to suffer, he says; "As the Father hath given me commandment, so I do." Again: "The cup which the Father hath given me, shall I not drink it?" And, at another time: "Father, if it be possible, let this cup pass from me; nevertheless, not as I will, but as thou wilt." And again: "Father, if this cup may not pass from me except I drink it, thy will be done." In all these passages it would rather appear that Christ endured death by the constraint of obedience, than by the inclination of his own free will.

Chapter IX

How it was of his own accord that he died, and what this means: "he was made obedient even unto death;" and: "for which cause God hath highly exalted him;" and: "I came not to do my own will;" and: "he spared not his own Son;" and: "not as I will, but as thou wilt."

Anselm. It seems to me that you do not rightly understand the difference between what he did at the demand of obedience, and what he suffered, not demanded by obedience, but inflicted on him, because he kept his obedience perfect.

Boso. I need to have you explain it more clearly.

Anselm. Why did the Jews persecute him even unto death?

Boso. For nothing else, but that, in word and in life, he invariably maintained truth and justice.

Anselm. I believe that God demands this of every rational being, and every being owes this in obedience to God.

Boso. We ought to acknowledge this.

Anselm. That man, therefore, owed this obedience to God the Father, humanity to Deity; and the Father claimed it from him.

Boso. There is no doubt of this.

Anselin. Now you see what he did, under the demand of obedience.

Boso. Very true, and I see also what infliction he endured, because he stood firm in obedience. For death was inflicted on him for his perseverance in obedience and he endured it; but I do not understand how it is that obedience did not demand this.

Anselm. Ought man to suffer death, if he had never sinned, or should God demand this of him?

Boso. It is on this account that we believe that man would not have been subject to death, and that God would not have exacted this of him; but I should like to hear the reason of the thing from you.

Anselm. You acknowledge that the intelligent creature was made holy, and for this purpose, viz., to be happy in the enjoyment of God.

Boso. Yes.

Anselm. You surely will not think it proper for God to make his creature miserable without fault, when he had created him holy that he might enjoy a state of blessedness. For it would be a miserable thing for man to die against his will.

Boso. It is plain that, if man had not sinned, God ought not to compel him to die.

Anselm. God did not, therefore, compel Christ to die; but he suffered death of his own will, not yielding up his life as an act of obedience, but on account of his obedience in maintaining holiness; for he held out so firmly in this obedience that he met death on account of it. It may, indeed be said, that the Father commanded him to die, when he enjoined that upon him on account of which he met death. It was in this sense, then, that "as the Father gave him the commandment, so he did, and the cup which He gave to him, he drank; and he was made obedient to the Father, even unto death;" and thus "he learned obedience from the things which he suffered," that is, how far obedience should be maintained. Now the word "didicit," which is used, can be understood in two ways. For either "didicit" is written for this: he caused others to learn; or it is used, because he did learn by experience what he had an understanding of before. Again, when the Apostle had said: "he humbled himself, being made obedient even unto death, and that the death of the cross," he added: "wherefore God also hath exalted him and given him a name, which is above every name." And this is similar to what David said: "he drank of the brook in the way, therefore did he lift up the head." For it is not meant that he could not have attained his exaltation in any other way but by obedience unto death; nor is it meant that his exaltation was conferred on him, only as a reward of his obedience (for he himself said before he suffered, that all things had been committed to him by the Father, and that all things belonging to the Father were his); but the expression is used because he had agreed with the Father and the Holy Spirit, that there was no other way to reveal to the world the height of his omnipotence, than by his death. For if a thing do not take place, except on condition of something else, it is not improperly said to occur by reason of that thing. For if we intend to do a thing, but mean to do something else first by means of which it may be done; when the first thing which we wish to do is done, if the result is such as we intended, it is properly said to be on account of the other; since that is now done which caused the delay; for it had been determined that the first thing should not be done without the other. If, for instance, I propose to cross a river only in a boat, though I can cross it in a boat or on horseback, and suppose that I delay crossing because the boat is gone; but if afterwards I cross, when the boat has returned, it may be properly said of me: the boat was ready, and therefore he crossed. And we not only use this form of expression, when it is by means of a thing which we desire should take place first, but also when we intend to do something else, not by means of that thing, but only after it. For if one delays taking food because he has not to-day attended the celebration of mass; when that has been done which he wished to do first, it is not improper to say to him: now take food, for you have now done that for which you delayed taking food. Far less, therefore, is the language strange, when Christ is said to be exalted on this account, because he endured death; for it was through this, and after this, that he determined to accomplish his exaltation. This may be understood also in the same way as that passage in which it is said that our Lord increased in wisdom, and in favor with God; not that this was really the case, but that he deported himself as if it were so. For he was exalted after his death, as if it were really on account of that. Moreover, that saying of his: "I came not to do mine own will, but the will of him that sent me," is precisely like that other saying: "My doctrine is not mine;" for what one does not have of himself, but of God, he ought not to call his own, but God's. Now no one has the truth which he teaches, or a holy will, of himself, but of God. Christ, therefore, came not to do his own will, but that of the Father; for his holy will was not derived from his humanity, but from his divinity. For that sentence: "God spared not his own Son, but gave him up for us all," means nothing more than that he did not rescue him. For there are found in the Bible many things like this. Again, when he says: "Father, if it be possible, let this cup pass from me; nevertheless not as I will, but as thou wilt;" and "If this cup may not pass from me, except I drink it, thy will be done;" he signifies by his own will the natural desire of safety, in accordance with which human nature shrank from the anguish of death. But he speaks of the will of the Father, not because the Father preferred the death of the Son to his life; but because the Father was not willing to rescue the human race, unless man were to do even as great a thing as was signified in the death of Christ. Since reason did not demand of another what he could not do, therefore, the Son says that he desires his own death. For he preferred to suffer, rather than that the human race should be lost; as if he were to say to the Father: "Since thou dost not desire the reconciliation of the world to take place in any other way, in this respect, I see that thou desirest my death; let thy will, therefore, be done, that is, let my death take place, so that the world may be reconciled to thee." For we often say that one desires a thing, because he does not choose something else, the choice of which would preclude the existence of that which he is said to desire; for instance, when we say that he who does not choose to close the window through which the draft is admitted which puts out the light, wishes the light to be extinguished. So the Father desired the death of the Son, because he was not willing that the world should be saved in any other way, except by man's doing so great a thing as that which I have mentioned. And this, since none other could accomplish it, availed as much with the Son, who so earnestly desired the salvation of man, as if the Father had commanded him to die; and, therefore, "as the Father gave him commandment, so he did, and the cup which the Father gave to him he drank, being obedient even unto death."

Chapter X

Likewise on the same topics; and how otherwise they can be correctly explained.

It is also a fair interpretation that it was by that same holy will by which the son wished to die for the salvation of the world, that the Father gave him commandment (yet not by compulsion), and the cup of suffering, and spared him not, but gave him up for us and desired his death; and that the Son himself was obedient even unto death, and learned obedience from the things which he suffered. For as with regard to that will which led him to a holy life, he did not have it as a human being of himself, but of the Father; so also that will by which he desired to die for the accomplishment of so great good, he could not have had but from the Father of lights, from whom is every good and perfect gift. And as the Father is said to draw by imparting an inclination, so there is nothing improper in asserting that he moves man. For as the Son says of the Father: "No man cometh to me except the Father draw him," he might as well have said, except he move him. In like manner, also, could he have declared: "No man layeth down his life for my sake, except the Father move or draw him." For since a man is drawn or moved by his will to that which he invariably chooses, it is not improper to say that God draws or moves him when he gives him this will. And in this drawing or impelling it is not to be understood that there is any constraint, but a free and grateful clinging to the holy will which has been given. If then it cannot be denied that the Father drew or moved the Son to death by giving him that will; who does not see that, in the same manner, he gave him commandment to endure death of his own accord and to take the cup, which he freely drank. And if it is right to say that the Son spared not himself, but gave himself for us of his own will, who will deny that it is right to say that the Father, of whom he had this will, did not spare him but gave him up for us, and desired his death? In this way, also, by following the will received from the Father invariably, and of his own accord, the Son became obedient to Him, even unto death; and learned obedience from the things which he suffered; that is, be learned how great was the work to be accomplished by obedience. For this is real and sincere obedience when a rational being, not of compulsion, but freely, follows the will received from

God. In other ways, also, we can properly explain the Father's desire that the Son should die, though these would appear sufficient. For as we say that he desires a thing who causes another to desire it; so, also, we say that he desires a thing who approves of the desire of another, though he does not cause that desire. Thus when we see a man who desires to endure pain with fortitude for the accomplishment of some good design; though we acknowledge that we wish to have him endure that pain, yet we do not choose, nor take pleasure in, his suffering, but in his choice. We are, also, accustomed to say that he who can prevent a thing but does not, desires the thing which he does not prevent. Since, therefore, the will of the Son pleased the Father, and he did not prevent him from choosing, or from fulfilling his choice, it is proper to say that he wished the Son to endure death so piously and for so great an object, though he was not pleased with his suffering. Moreover, he said that the cup must not pass from him, except he drank it, not because he could not have escaped death had he chosen to; but because, as has been said, the world could not otherwise be saved; and it was his fixed choice to suffer death, rather than that the world should not be saved. It was for *this* reason, also, that he used those words, viz., to teach the human race that there was no other salvation for them but by his death; and not to show that he had no power at all to avoid death. For whatsoever things are said of him, similar to these which have been mentioned, they are all to be explained in accordance with the belief that he died, not by compulsion, but of free choice. For he was omnipotent, and it is said of him, when he was offered up, that he desired it. And he says himself: "I lay down my life that I may take it again; no man taketh it from me, but I lay it down of myself; I have power to lay it down, and I have power to take it again." A man cannot, therefore, be properly said to have been driven to a thing which he does of his own power and will.

Boso. But this simple fact, that God allows him to be so treated, even if he were willing, does not seem becoming for such a Father in respect to such a Son.

Anselm. Yes, it is of all things most proper that such a Father should acquiesce with such a Son in his desire, if it be praiseworthy as relates to the honor of God, and useful for man's salvation, which would not otherwise be effected.

Boso. The question which still troubles us is, how the death of the Son can be proved reasonable and necessary. For otherwise, it does not seem that the Son ought to desire it, or the Father compel or permit it. For the question is, why God could not save man in some other way, and if so, why he wished to do it in this way? For it both seems unbecoming for God to have saved man in this way; and it is not clear how the death of the Son avails for the salvation of man. For it is a strange thing if God so delights in, or requires, the blood of the innocent, that he neither chooses, nor is able, to spare the guilty without the sacrifice of the innocent.

Anselm. Since, in this inquiry, you take the place of those who are unwilling to believe anything not previously proved by reason, I wish to have it understood between us that we do not admit anything in the least unbecoming to be ascribed to the Deity, and that we do not reject the *smallest* reason if it be not opposed by a greater. For as it is impossible to attribute anything in the least unbecoming to God; so any reason, however small, if not overbalanced by a greater, has the force of necessity.

Boso. In this matter, I accept nothing more willingly than that this agreement should be preserved between us in common.

Anselm. The question concerns only the incarnation of God, and those things which we believe with regard to his taking human nature.

Boso. It is so.

Anselm. Let us suppose, then, that the incarnation of God, and the things that we affirm of him as man, had never taken place; and be it agreed between us that man was made for happiness, which cannot be attained in this life, and that no being can ever arrive at happiness, save by freedom from sin, and that no man passes this life without sin. Let us take for granted, also, the other things, the belief of which is necessary for eternal salvation.

Boso. I grant it; for in these there is nothing which seems unbecoming or impossible for God.

Anselm. Therefore, in order that man may attain happiness, remission of sin is necessary.

Boso. We all hold this.

Chapter XI

What it is to sin, and to make satisfaction for sin.

Anselm. We must needs inquire, therefore, in what manner God puts away men's sins; and, in order to do this more plainly, let us first consider what it is to sin, and what it is to make satisfaction for sin.

Boso. It is yours to explain and mine to listen.

Anselm. If man or angel always rendered to God his due, he would never sin.

Boso. I cannot deny that.

Anselm. Therefore to sin is nothing else than not to render to God his due.

Boso. What is the debt which we owe to God?

Anselm. Every wish of a rational creature should be subject to the will of God.

Boso. Nothing is more true.

Anselm. This is the debt which man and angel owe to God, and no one who pays this debt commits sin; but every one who does not pay it sins. This is justice, or uprightness of will, which makes a being just or upright in heart, that is, in will; and this is the sole and complete debt of honor which we owe to God, and which God requires of us. For it is such a will only, when it can be exercised, that does works pleasing to God; and when this will cannot be exercised, it is pleasing of itself alone, since without it no work is acceptable. He who does not render this honor which is due to God, robs God of his own and dishonors him; and this is sin. Moreover, so long as he does not restore what he has taken away, he remains in fault; and it will not suffice merely to restore what has been taken away, but, considering the contempt offered, he ought to restore more than he took away. For as one who imperils another's safety does not enough by merely restoring his safety, without making some compensation for the anguish incurred; so he who violates another's honor does not enough by merely rendering honor again, but must, according to the extent of the injury done, make restoration in some way satisfactory to the person whom he has dishonored. We must also observe that when any one pays what he has unjustly taken away, he ought to give something which could not have been demanded of him, had he not stolen what belonged to another. So then, every one who sins ought to pay back the honor of which he has robbed God; and this is the satisfaction which every sinner owes to God.

Boso. Since we have determined to follow reason in all these things, I am unable to bring any objection against them, although you somewhat startle me.

Chapter XII

Whether it were proper for God to put away sins by compassion alone, without any payment of debt.

Anselm. Let us return and consider whether it were proper for God to put away sins by compassion alone, without any payment of the honor taken from him.

Boso. I do not see why it is not proper.

Anselm. To remit sin in this manner is nothing else than not to punish; and since it is not right to cancel sin without compensation or punishment; if it be not punished, then is it passed by undischarged.

Boso. What you say is reasonable.

Anselm. It is not fitting for God to pass over anything in his kingdom undischarged.

Boso. If I wish to oppose this, I fear to sin.

Anselm. It is, therefore, not proper for God thus to pass over sin unpunished.

Boso. Thus it follows.

Anselm. There is also another thing which follows if sin be passed by unpunished, viz., that with God there will be no difference between the guilty and the not guilty; and this is unbecoming to God.

Boso. I cannot deny it.

Anselm. Observe this also. Every one knows that justice to man is regulated by law, so that, according to the requirements of law, the measure of award is bestowed by God.

Boso. This is our belief.

Anselm. But if sin is neither paid for nor punished, it is subject to no law.

Boso. I cannot conceive it to be otherwise.

Anselm. Injustice, therefore, if it is cancelled by compassion alone, is more free than justice, which seems very inconsistent. And to these is also added a further incongruity, viz., that it makes injustice like God. For as God is subject to no law, so neither is injustice.

Boso. I cannot withstand your reasoning. But when God commands us in every case to forgive those who trespass against us, it seems inconsistent to enjoin a thing upon us which it is not proper for him to do himself.

Anselm. There is no inconsistency in God's commanding us not to take upon ourselves what belongs to Him alone. For to execute vengeance belongs to none but Him who is Lord of all; for when the powers of the world rightly accomplish this end, God himself does it who appointed them for the purpose.

Boso. You have obviated the difficulty which I thought to exist; but there is another to which I would like to have your answer. For since God is so free as to be subject to no law, and to the judgment of no one, and is so merciful as that nothing more merciful can be conceived; and nothing is right or fit save as he wills; it seems a strange thing for us to say that he is wholly unwilling or unable to put away an injury done to himself, when we are wont to apply to him for indulgence with regard to those offences which we commit against others.

Anselm. What you say of God's liberty and choice and compassion is true; but we ought so to interpret these things as that they may not seem to interfere with His dignity. For there is no liberty except as regards what is best or fitting; nor should that be called mercy which does anything improper for the Divine character. Moreover, when it is said that what God wishes is just, and that what He does not wish is unjust, we must not understand that if God wished anything improper it would be just, simply because he wished it. For if God wishes to lie, we must not conclude that it is right to lie, but rather that he is not God. For no will can ever wish to lie, unless truth in it is impaired, nay, unless the will itself be impaired by forsaking truth. When, then, it is said: "If God wishes to lie," the meaning is simply this: "If the nature of God is such as that he wishes to lie;" and, therefore, it does not follow that falsehood is right, except it be understood in the same manner as when we speak of two impossible things: "If this be true, then that follows; because neither *this* nor *that* is true;" as if a man should say: "Supposing water to be dry, and fire to be moist;" for neither is the case. Therefore, with regard to these things, to speak the whole truth: If God desires a thing, it is right that he should desire that which involves no unfitness. For if God chooses that it should rain, it is right that it should rain; and if he desires that any man should die, then is it right that he should die. Wherefore, if it be not fitting for God to do anything unjustly, or out of course, it does not belong to his liberty or compassion or will to let the sinner go unpunished who makes no return to God of what the sinner has defrauded him.

Boso. You remove from me every possible objection which I had thought of bringing against you.

Anselm. Yet observe why it is not fitting for God to do this.

Boso. I listen readily to whatever you say.

Chapter XIII

How nothing less was to be endured, in the order of things, than that the creature should take away the honor due the Creator and not restore what he takes away.

Anselm. In the order of things, there is nothing less to be endured than that the creature should take away the honor due the Creator, and not restore what he has taken away.

Boso. Nothing is more plain than this.

Anselm. But there is no greater injustice suffered than that by which so great an evil must be endured.

Boso. This, also, is plain.

Anselm. I think, therefore, that you will not say that God ought to endure a thing than which no greater injustice is suffered, viz., that the creature should not restore to God what he has taken away.

Boso. No; I think it should be wholly denied.

Anselm. Again, if there is nothing greater or better than God, there is nothing more just than supreme justice, which maintains God's honor in the arrangement of things, and which is nothing else but God himself.

Boso. There is nothing clearer than this.

Anselm. Therefore God maintains nothing with more justice than the honor of his own dignity.

Boso. I must agree with you.

Anselm. Does it seem to you that he wholly preserves it, if he allows himself to be so defrauded of it as that he should neither receive satisfaction nor punish the one defrauding him.

Boso. I dare not say so.

Anselni. Therefore the honor taken away must be repaid, or punishment must follow; otherwise, either God will not be just to himself, or he will be weak in respect to both parties; and this it is impious even to think of.

Boso. I think that nothing more reasonable can be said.

Chapter XIV

How the honor of God exists in the punishment of the wicked.

Boso. But I wish to hear from you whether the punishment of the sinner is an honor to God, or how it is an honor. For if the punishment of the sinner is not for God's honor when the sinner does not pay what he took away, but is punished, God loses his honor so that he cannot recover it. And this seems in contradiction to the things which have been said.

Anselm. It is impossible for God to lose his honor; for either the sinner pays his debt of his own accord, or, if he refuse, God takes it from him. For either man renders due submission to God of his own will, by avoiding sin or making payment, or else God subjects him to himself by torments, even against man's will, and thus shows that he is the Lord of man, though man refuses to acknowledge it of his own accord. And here we must observe that as man in sinning takes away what belongs to God, so God in punishing gets in return what pertains to man. For not only does that belong to a man which he has in present possession, but also that which it is in his power to have. Therefore, since man was so made as to be able to attain happiness by avoiding sin; if, on account of his sin, he is deprived of happiness and every good, he repays from his own inheritance what he has stolen, though he repay it against his will. For although God does not apply what he takes away to any object of his own, as man transfers the money which he has taken from another to his own use; yet what he takes away serves the purpose of his own honor, for this very reason, that it is taken away. For by this act he shows that the sinner and all that pertains to him are under his subjection.

Chapter XV

Whether God suffers his honor to be violated even in the least degree.

Boso. What you say satisfies me. But there is still another point which I should like to have you answer. For if, as you make out, God ought to sustain his own honor, why does he allow it to be violated even in the least degree? For what is in any way made liable to injury is not entirely and perfectly preserved.

Anselm. Nothing can be added to or taken from the honor of God. For this honor which belongs to him is in no way subject to injury or change. But as the individual creature preserves, naturally or by reason, the condition belonging, and, as it were, allotted to him, he is said to obey and honor God; and to this, rational nature, which possesses intelligence, is especially bound. And when the being chooses what he ought, he honors God; not by bestowing anything upon him, but because he brings himself freely under God's will and disposal, and maintains his own condition in the universe, and the beauty of the universe itself, as far as in him lies. But when he does not choose what he ought, he dishonors God, as far as the being himself is concerned, because he does not submit himself freely to God's disposal. And he disturbs the order and beauty of the universe, as relates to himself, although he cannot injure nor tarnish the power and majesty of God. For if those things which are held together in the circuit of the heavens desire to be elsewhere than under the heavens, or to be further removed from the heavens, there is no place where they can be but under the heavens, nor can they fly from the heavens without also approaching them. For both whence and whither and in what way they go, they are still under the heavens; and if they are at a greater distance from one part of them, they are only so much nearer to the opposite part. And so, though man or evil angel refuse to submit to the Divine will and appointment, yet he cannot escape it; for if he wishes to fly from a will that commands, he falls into the power of a will that punishes. And if you ask whither he goes, it is only under the permission of that will; and even this wayward choice or action of his becomes subservient, under infinite wisdom, to the order and beauty of the universe before spoken of. For when it is understood that God brings good out of many forms of evil, then the satisfaction for sin freely given, or if this be not given, the exaction of punishment, hold their own place and orderly beauty in the same universe. For if Divine wisdom were not to insist upon things, when wickedness tries to disturb the right appointment, there would be, in the very universe which God ought to control, an unseemliness springing from the violation of the beauty of arrangement, and God would appear to be deficient in his management. And these two things are not only unfitting, but consequently impossible; so that satisfaction or punishment must needs follow every sin.

Boso. You have relieved my objection.

Anselm. It is then plain that no one can honor or dishonor God, as he is in himself; but the creature, as far as he is concerned, appears to do this when he submits or opposes his will to the will of God.

Boso. I know of nothing which can be said against this.

Anselm. Let me add something to it.

Boso. Go on, until I am weary of listening.

Chapter XVI

The reason why the number of angels who fell must be made up from men.

Anselm. It was proper that God should design to make up for the number of angels that fell, from human nature which he created without sin.

Boso. This is a part of our belief, but still I should like to have some reason for it.

Anselm. You mistake me, for we intended to discuss only the incarnation of the Deity, and here you are bringing in other questions.

Boso. Be not angry with me; "for the Lord loveth a cheerful giver;" and no one shows better how cheerfully he gives what he promises, than he who gives more than he promises; therefore, tell me freely what I ask.

Anselm. There is no question that intelligent nature, which finds its happiness, both now and forever, in the contemplation of God, was foreseen by him in a certain reasonable and complete number, so that there would be an unfitness in its being either less or greater. For either God did not know in what number it was best to create rational beings, which is false; or, if he did know, then he appointed such a number as he perceived was most fitting. Wherefore, either the angels who fell were made so as to be within that number; or, since they were out of that number, they could not continue to exist, and so fell of necessity. But this last is an absurd idea.

Boso. The truth which you set forth is plain.

Anselm. Therefore, since they ought to be of that number, either their number should of necessity be made up, or else rational nature, which was foreseen as perfect in number, will remain incomplete. But this cannot be.

Boso. Doubtless, then, the number must be restored.

Anselm. But this restoration can only be made from human beings, since there is no other source.

Chapter XVII

How other angels cannot take the place of those who fell.

Boso. Why could not they themselves be restored, or other angels substituted for them?

Anselm. When you shall see the difficulty of our restoration, you will understand the impossibility of theirs. But other angels cannot be substituted for them on this account (to pass over its apparent inconsistency with the completeness of the first creation), because they ought to be such as the former angels would have been, had they never sinned. But the first angels in that case would have persevered without ever witnessing the punishment of sin; which, in respect to the others who were substituted for them after their fall, was impossible. For two beings who stand firm in truth are not equally deserving of praise, if one has never seen the punishment of sin, and the other forever witnesses its eternal reward. For it must not for a moment be supposed that good angels are upheld by the fall of evil angels, but by their own virtue. For, as they would have been condemned together, had the good sinned with the bad, so, had the unholy stood firm with the holy, they would have been likewise upheld. For, if, without the fall of a part, the rest could not be upheld, it would follow, either that none could ever be upheld, or else that it was necessary for some one to fall, in order by his punishment to uphold the rest; but either of these suppositions is absurd. Therefore, had all stood, all would have been upheld in the same manner as those who stood; and this manner I explained, as well as I could, when treating of the reason why God did not bestow perseverance upon the devil.

Boso. You have proved that the evil angels must be restored from the human race; and from this reasoning it appears that the number of men chosen will not be less than that of fallen angels. But show, if you can, whether it will be greater.

Chapter XVIII

Whether there will be more holy men than evil angels.

Anselm. If the angels, before any of them fell, existed in that perfect number of which we have spoken, then men were only made to supply the place of the lost angels; and it is plain that their number will not be greater. But if that number were not found in all the angels together, then both the loss and the original deficiency must be made up from men, and more men will be chosen than there were fallen angels. And so we shall say that men were made not only to restore the diminished number, but also to complete the imperfect number.

Boso. Which is the better theory, that angels were originally made perfect in number or that they were not?

Anselm. I will state my views.

Boso. I cannot ask more of you.

Anselm. If man was created after the fall of evil angels, as some understand the account in Genesis, I do not think that I can prove from this either of these suppositions positively. For it is possible, I think, that the angels should have been created perfect in number, and that afterwards man was created to complete their number when it had been lessened; and it is also possible that they were not perfect in number, because God deferred completing the number, as he does even now, determining in his own time to create man. Wherefore, either God would only complete that which was not yet perfect, or, if it were also diminished, He would restore it. But if the whole creation took place at once, and those days in which Moses appears to describe a successive creation are not to be understood like such days as ours, I cannot see how angels could have been created perfect in number. Since, if it were so, it seems to me that some, either men or angels, would fall immediately, else in heaven's empire there would be more than the complete number required. If, therefore, all things were created at one and the same time, it should seem that angels, and the first two human beings, formed an incomplete number, so that, if no angel fell, the deficiency alone should be made up, but if any fell, the lost part should be restored; and that human nature, which had stood firm, though weaker than that of angels, might, as it were, justify God, and put the devil to silence, if he were to attribute his fall to weakness. And in case human nature fell, much more would it justify God against the devil, and even against itself, because, though made far weaker and of a mortal race, yet, in the elect, it would rise from its weakness to an estate exalted above that from which the devil was fallen, as far as good angels, to whom it should be equal, were advanced after the overthrow of the evil, because they persevered. From these reasons, I am rather inclined to the belief that there was not, originally, that complete number of angels necessary to perfect the celestial state; since, supposing that man and angels were not created at the same time, this is possible; and it would follow of necessity, if they were created at the same time, which is the opinion of the majority, because we read: "He, who liveth forever, created all things at once." But if the perfection of the created universe is to be understood as consisting, not so much in the number of beings, as in the number of natures; it follows that human nature was either made to consummate this perfection, or that it was superfluous, which we should not dare affirm of the nature of the smallest reptile. Wherefore, then, it was made for itself, and not merely to restore the number of beings possessing another nature. From which it is plain that, even had no angel fallen, men would yet have had their place in the celestial kingdom. And hence it follows that there was not a perfect number of angels, even before a part fell; otherwise, of necessity some men or angels must fall, because it would be impossible that any should continue beyond the perfect number.

Boso. You have not labored in vain.

Anselm. There is, also, as I think, another reason which supports, in no small degree, the opinion that angels were not created perfect in number.

Boso. Let us hear it.

Anselm. Had a perfect number of angels been created, and had man been made only to fill the place of the lost angels, it is plain that, had not some angels fallen from their happiness, man would never have, been exalted to it.

Boso. We are agreed.

Anselm. But if any one shall ask: "Since the elect rejoice as much over the fall of angels as over their own exaltation, because the one can never take place without the other; how can they be justified in this unholy joy, or how shall we say that angels are restored by the substitution of men, if they (the angels) would have remained free from this fault, had they not fallen, viz., from rejoicing over the fall of others?" We reply: Cannot men be made free from this fault? nay, how ought they to be happy with this fault? With what temerity, then, do we say that God neither wishes nor is able to make this substitution without this fault!

Boso. Is not the case similar to that of the Gentiles who were called unto faith, because the Jews rejected it?

Anselm. No; for had the Jews all believed, yet the Gentiles would have been called; for "in every nation he that feareth God and worketh righteousness is accepted of him." But since the Jews despised the apostles, this was the immediate occasion of their turning to the Gentiles.

Boso. I see no way of opposing you.

Anselm. Whence does that joy which one has over another's fall seem to arise?

Boso. Whence, to be sure, but from the fact that each individual will be certain that, had not another fallen, he would never have attained the place where he now is?

Anselm. If, then, no one had this certainty, there would be no cause for one to rejoice over the doom of another.

Boso. So it appears.

Anselm. Think you that any one of them can have this certainty, if their number shall far exceed that of those who fell?

Boso. I certainly cannot think that any one would or ought to have it. For how can any one know whether he were created to restore the part diminished, or to make up that which was not yet complete in the number necessary to constitute the state? But all are sure that they were made with a view to the perfection of that kingdom.

Anselm. If, then, there shall be a larger number than that of the fallen angels, no one can or ought to know that he would not have attained this height but for another's fall.

Boso. That is true.

Anselm. No one, therefore, will have cause to rejoice over the perdition of another.

Boso. So it appears.

Anselm. Since, then, we see that if there are more men elected than the number of fallen angels, the incongruity will not follow which must follow if there are not more men elected; and since it is impossible that there should be anything incongruous in that celestial state, it becomes a necessary fact that angels were not made perfect in number, and that there will be more happy men than doomed angels.

Boso. I see not how this can be denied.

Anselm. I think that another reason can be brought to support this opinion.

Boso. You ought then to present it.

Anselm. We believe that the material substance of the world must be renewed, and that this will not take place until the number of the elect is accomplished, and that happy kingdom made perfect, and that after its completion there will be no change. Whence it may be reasoned that God planned to perfect both at the same time, in order that the inferior nature, which knew not God, might not be perfected before the superior nature which ought to enjoy God; and that the inferior, being renewed at the same time with the superior, might, as it were, rejoice in its own way; yes, that every creature having so glorious and excellent a consummation, might delight in its Creator and in itself, in turn, rejoicing always after its own manner, so that what the will effects in the rational nature of its own accord, this also the irrational creature naturally shows by the arrangement of God. For we are wont to rejoice in the fame of our ancestors, as when on the birthdays of the saints we delight with festive triumph, rejoicing in their honor. And this opinion derives support from the fact that, had not Adam sinned, God might yet put off the completion of that state until the number of men which he designed should be made out, and men themselves be transferred, so to speak, to an immortal state of bodily existence. For they had in paradise a kind of immortality, that is, a power not to die, but since it was possible for them to die, this power was not immortal, as if, indeed, they had not been capable of death. But if God determined to bring to perfection, at one and the same time, that intelligent and happy state and this earthly and irrational nature; it follows that either that state was not complete in the number of angels before the destruction of the wicked, but God was waiting to complete it by men, when he should renovate the material nature of the world; or that, if that kingdom were perfect in number, it was not in confirmation, and its confirmation must be deferred, even had no one sinned, until that renewal of the world to which we look forward; or that, if that confirmation could not be deferred so long, the renewal of the world must be hastened that both events might take place at the same time. But that God should determine to renew the world immediately after it was made, and to destroy in the very beginning those things which after this renewal would not exist, before any reason appeared for their creation, is simply absurd. It therefore follows that, since angels were not complete in number, their confirmation will not be long deferred on this account, because the renewal of a world just created ought soon to take place, for this is not fitting. But that God should wish to put off their confirmation to the future renewing of the world seems improper, since he so quickly accomplished it in some, and since we know that in regard to our first parents, if they had not sinned as they did, he would have confirmed them, as well as the angels who persevered. For, although not yet advanced to that equality with angels to which men were to attain, when the number taken from among them was complete; yet, had they preserved their original holiness, so as not to have sinned though tempted, they would have been confirmed, with all their offspring, so as never more to sin; just as when they were conquered by sin, they were so weakened as to be unable, in themselves, to live afterwards without sinning. For who dares affirm that wickedness is more powerful to bind a man in servitude, after he has yielded to it at the first persuasion, than holiness to confirm him in liberty when he has adhered to it in the original trial? For as human nature, being included in the person of our first parents, was in them wholly won over to sin (with the single exception of that man whom God being able to create from a virgin was equally able to save from the sin of Adam), so had they not sinned, human nature would have wholly conquered. It therefore remains that the celestial state was not complete in its original number, but must be completed from among men.

Boso. What you say seems very reasonable to me. But what shall we think of that which is said respecting God: "He hath appointed the bounds of the people according to the number of the children of Israel;" which some, because for the expression "children of Israel" is found sometimes "angels of God," explain in this way, that the number of elect men taken should be understood as equal to that of good angels?

Anselm. This is not discordant with the previous opinion, if it be not certain that the number of angels who fell is the same as that of those who stood. For if there be more elect than evil angels, and elect men must needs be substituted for the evil angels, and it is possible for them to equal the number of the good angels, in that case there will be more holy men than evil angels. But remember with what condition I undertook to answer your inquiry, viz., that if I say anything not upheld by greater authority, though I appear to demonstrate it, yet it should be received with no further certainty than as my opinion for the present, until God makes some clearer revelation to me. For I am sure that, if I say anything which plainly opposes the Holy Scriptures, it is false; and if I am aware of it, I will no longer hold it. But if, with regard to subjects in which opposite opinions may be held without hazard, as that, for instance, which we now discuss; for if we know not whether there are to be more men elected than the number of the lost angels, and incline to either of these opinions rather than the other, I think the soul is not in danger; if, I say, in questions like this, we explain the Divine words so as to make them favor different sides, and there is nowhere found anything to decide, beyond doubt, the opinion that should be held, I think there is no censure to be given. As to the passage which you spoke of: "He hath determined the bounds of the people (or tribes) according to the number of the angels of God;" or as another translation has it: "according to the number of the children of Israel;" since both translations either mean the same thing, or are different, without contradicting each other, we may understand that good angels only are intended by both expressions, "angels of God," and "children of Israel," or that elect men only are meant, or that both angels and elect men are included, even the whole celestial kingdom. Or by angels of God may be understood holy angels only, and by children of Israel, holy men only; or, by children of Israel, angels only, and by angels of God, holy men. If good angels are intended in both expressions, it is the same as if only "angels of God" had been used; but if the whole heavenly kingdom were included, the meaning is, that a people, that is, the throng of elect men, is to be taken, or that there will be a people in this stage of existence, until the appointed number of that kingdom, not yet completed, shall be made up from among men. But I do not now see why angels only, or even angels and holy men together, are meant by the expression "children of Israel"; for it is not improper to call holy men "children of Israel," as they are called "sons of Abraham." And they can also properly be called "angels of God," because they imitate the life of angels, and they are promised in heaven a likeness to and equality with angels, and all who live holy lives are angels of God. Therefore the confessors or martyrs are so called; for he who declares and bears witness to the truth, he is a messenger of God, that is, his angel. And if a wicked man is called a devil, as our Lord says of Judas, because they are alike in malice; why should not a good man be called an angel, because he follows holiness? Wherefore I think we may say that God hath appointed the bounds of the people according to the number of elect men, because men will exist and there will be a natural increase among them, until the number of elect men is accomplished; and when that occurs, the birth of men, which takes place in this life, will cease. But if by "angels of God" we only understand holy angels, and by "children of Israel" only holy men; it may be explained in two ways: that "God hath appointed the bounds of the people according to the number of the angels of God," viz., either that so great a people, that is, so many men, will be taken as there are holy angels of God, or that a people will continue to exist upon earth, until the number of angels is completed from among men. And I think there is no other possible method of explanation: "he hath appointed the bounds of the people according to the number of the children of Israel," that is, that there will continue to be a people in this stage of existence, as I said above, until the number of holy men is completed. And we infer from either translation that as many men will be taken as there were angels who remained steadfast. Yet, although lost angels must have their ranks filled by men, it does not follow that the number of lost angels was equal to that of those who persevered. But if any one affirms this, he will have to find means of invalidating the reasons given above, which prove, I think, that there was not among angels, before the fall, that perfect number before mentioned, and that there are more men to be saved than the number of evil angels.

Boso. I by no means regret that I urged you to these remarks about the angels, for it has not been for nought. Now let us return from our digression.

Chapter XIX

How man cannot be saved without satisfaction for sin.

Anselm. It was fitting for God to fill the places of the fallen angels from among men.

Boso. That is certain.

Anselm. Therefore there ought to be in the heavenly empire as many men taken as substitutes for the angels as would correspond with the number whose place they shall take, that is, as many as there are good angels now; otherwise they who fell will not be restored, and it will follow that God either could not accomplish the good which he begun, or he will repent of having undertaken it; either of which is absurd.

Boso. Truly it is fitting that men should be equal with good angels.

Anselm. Have good angels ever sinned?

Boso. No.

Anselm. Can you think that man, who has sinned, and never made satisfaction to God for his sin, but only been suffered to go unpunished, may become the equal of an angel who has never sinned?

Boso. These words I can both think of and utter, but can no more perceive their meaning than I can make truth out of falsehood.

Anselm. Therefore it is not fitting that God should take sinful man without an atonement, in substitution for lost angels; for truth will not suffer man thus to be raised to an equality with holy beings.

Boso. Reason shows this.

Anselm. Consider, also, leaving out the question of equality with the angels, whether God ought, under such circumstances, to raise man to the same or a similar kind of happiness as that which he had before he sinned.

Boso. Tell your opinion, and I will attend to it as well as I can.

Anselm. Suppose a rich man possessed a choice pearl which had never been defiled, and which could not be taken from his hands without his permission; and that he determined to commit it to the treasury of his dearest and most valuable possessions.

Boso. I accept your supposition.

Anselm. What if he should allow it to be struck from his hand and cast in the mire, though he might have prevented it; and afterwards taking it all soiled by the mire and unwashed, should commit it again to his beautiful and loved casket; will you consider him a wise man?

Boso. How can I? for would it not be far better to keep and preserve his pearl pure, than to have it polluted?

Anselm. Would not God be acting like this, who held man in paradise, as it were in his own hand, without sin, and destined to the society of angels, and allowed the devil, inflamed with envy, to cast him into the mire of sin, though truly with man's consent? For, had God chosen to restrain the devil, the devil could not have tempted man. Now I say, would not God be acting like this, should he restore man, stained with the defilement of sin, unwashed, that is, without any satisfaction, and always to remain so; should He restore him at once to paradise, from which he had been thrust out?

Boso. I dare not deny the aptness of your comparison, were God to do this, and therefore do not admit that he can do this. For it should seem either that he could not accomplish what he designed, or else that he repented of his good intent, neither of which things is possible with God.

Anselm. Therefore, consider it settled that, without satisfaction, that is, without voluntary payment of the debt, God can neither pass by the sin unpunished, nor can the sinner attain that happiness, or happiness like that, which he had before he sinned; for man cannot in this way be restored, or become such as he was before he sinned.

Boso. I am wholly unable to refute your reasoning. But what say you to this: that we pray God, "put away our sins from us," and every nation prays the God of its faith to put away its sins. For, if we pay our debt, why do we pray God to put it away? Is not God unjust to demand what has already been paid? But if we do not make payment, why do we supplicate in vain that he will do what he cannot do, because it is unbecoming?

Anselm. He who does not pay says in vain: "Pardon"; but he who pays makes supplication, because prayer is properly connected with the payment; for God owes no man anything, but every creature owes God; and, therefore, it does not become man to treat with God as with an equal. But of this it is not now needful for me to answer you. For when you think why Christ died, I think you will see yourself the answer to your question.

Boso. Your reply with regard to this matter suffices me for the present. And, moreover, you have so clearly shown that no man can attain happiness in sin, or be freed from sin without satisfaction for the trespass, that, even were I so disposed, I could not doubt it.

Chapter XX

That satisfaction ought to be proportionate to guilt; and that man is of himself unable to accomplish this.

Anselm. Neither, I think, will you doubt this, that satisfaction should be proportionate to guilt.

Boso. Otherwise sin would remain in a manner exempt from control (*inordinatum*), which cannot be, for God leaves nothing uncontrolled in his kingdom. But this is determined, that even the smallest unfitness is impossible with God.

Anselm. Tell me, then, what payment you make God for your sin?

Boso. Repentance, a broken and contrite heart, self-denial, various bodily sufferings, pity in giving and forgiving, and obedience.

Anselm. What do you give to God in all these?

Boso. Do I not honor God, when, for his love and fear, in heartfelt contrition I give up worldly joy, and despise, amid abstinence and toils, the delights and ease of this life, and submit obediently to him, freely bestowing my possessions in giving to and releasing others?

Anselm. When you render anything to God which you owe him, irrespective of your past sin, you should not reckon this as the debt which you owe for sin. But you owe God every one of those things which you have mentioned. For, in this mortal state, there should be such love and such desire of attaining the true end of your being, which is the meaning of prayer, and such grief that you have not yet reached this object, and such fear lest you fail of it, that you should find joy in nothing which does not help you or give encouragement of your success. For you do not deserve to have a thing which you do not love and desire for its own sake, and the want of which at present, together with the great danger of never getting it, causes you no grief. This also requires one to avoid ease and worldly pleasures such as seduce the mind from real rest and pleasure, except so far as you think suffices for the accomplishment of that object. But you ought to view the gifts which you bestow as a part of your debt, since you know that what you give comes not from yourself, but from him whose servant both you are and he also to whom you give. And nature herself teaches you to do to your fellow servant, man to man, as you would be done by; and that he who will not bestow what he has ought not to receive what he has not. Of forgiveness, indeed, I speak briefly, for, as we said above, vengeance in no sense belongs to you, since you are not your own, nor is he who injures you yours or his, but you are both the servants of one Lord, made by him out of nothing. And if you avenge yourself upon your fellow servant, you proudly assume judgment over him when it is the peculiar right of God, the judge of all. But what do you give to God by your obedience, which is not owed him already, since he demands from you all that you are and have and can become?

Boso. Truly I dare not say that in all these things I pay any portion of my debt to God.

Anselm. How then do you pay God for your transgression?

Boso. If in justice I owe God myself and all my powers, even when I do not sin, I have nothing left to render to him for my sin.

Anselm. What will become of you then? How will you be saved?

Boso. Merely looking at your arguments, I see no way of escape. But, turning to my belief, I hope through Christian faith, "which works by love," that I may be saved, and the more, since we read that if the sinner turns from his iniquity and does what is right, all his transgressions shall be forgotten.

Anselm. This is only said of those who either looked for Christ before his coming, or who believe in him since he has appeared. But we set aside Christ and his religion as if they did not exist, when we proposed to inquire whether his coming were necessary to man's salvation.

Boso. We did so.

Anselm. Let us then proceed by reason simply.

Boso. Though you bring me into straits, yet I very much wish you to proceed as you have begun.

Chapter XXI

How great a burden sin is.

Anselm. Suppose that you did not owe any of those things which you have brought up as possible payment for your sin, let us inquire whether they can satisfy for a sin so small as one look contrary to the will of God.

Boso. Did I not hear you question the thing, I should suppose that a single repentant feeling on my part would blot out this sin.

Anselm. You have not as yet estimated the great burden of sin.

Boso. Show it me then.

Anselm. If you should find yourself in the sight of God, and one said to you: "Look thither;" and God, on the other hand, should say: "It is not my will that you should look;" ask your own heart what there is in all existing things which would make it right for you to give that look contrary to the will of God.

Boso. I can find no motive which would make it right; unless, indeed I am so situated as to make it necessary for me eithcr to do this, or some greater sin.

Anselm. Put away all such necessity, and ask with regard to this sin only whether you can do it even for your own salvation.

Boso. I see plainly that I cannot.

Anselm. Not to detain you too long; what if it were necessary either that the whole universe, except God himself, should perish and fall back into nothing, or else that you should do so small a thing against the will of God?

Boso. When I consider the action itself, it appears very slight; but when I view it as contrary to the will of God, I know of nothing so grievous, and of no loss that will compare with it; but sometimes we oppose another's will without blame in order to preserve his property, so that afterwards he is glad that we opposed him.

Anselm. This is in the case of man, who often does not know what is useful for him, or cannot make up his loss; but God is in want of nothing, and, should all things perish, can restore them as easily as he created them.

Boso. I must confess that I ought not to oppose the will of God even to preserve the whole creation.

Anselm. What if there were more worlds as full of beings as this?

Boso. Were they increased to an infinite extent, and held before me in like manner, my reply would be the same.

Anselm. You cannot answer more correctly, but consider, also, should it happen that you gave the look contrary to God's will, what payment you can make for this sin?

Boso. I can only repeat what I said before.

Anselm. So heinous is our sin whenever we knowingly oppose the will of God even in the slightest thing; since we are always in his sight, and he always enjoins it upon us not to sin.

Boso. I cannot deny it.

Anselm. Therefore you make no satisfaction unless you restore something greater than the amount of that obligation, which should restrain you from committing the sin.

Boso. Reason seems to demand this, and to make the contrary wholly impossible.

Anselm. Even God cannot raise to happiness any being bound at all by the debt of sin, because He ought not to.

Boso. This decision is most weighty.

Anselm. Listen to an additional reason which makes it no less difficult for man to be reconciled to God.

Boso. This alone would drive me to despair, were it not for the consolation of faith.

Anselm. But listen.

Boso. Say on.

Chapter XXII

What contempt man brought upon God, when he allowed himself to be conquered by the devil; for which he can make no satisfaction.

Anselm. Man being made holy was placed in paradise, as it were in the place of God, between God and the devil, to conquer the devil by not yielding to his temptation, and so to vindicate the honor of God and put the devil to shame, because that man, though weaker and dwelling upon earth, should not sin though tempted by the devil, while the devil, though stronger and in heaven, sinned without any to tempt him. And when man could have easily effected this, he, without compulsion and of his own accord, allowed himself to be brought over to the will of the devil, contrary to the will and honor of God.

Boso. To what would you bring me?

Anselm. Decide for yourself if it be not contrary to the honor of God for man to be reconciled to Him, with this calumnious reproach still heaped upon God; unless man first shall have honored God by overcoming the devil, as he dishonored him in yielding to the devil. Now the victory ought to be of this kind, that, as in strength and immortal vigor, he freely yielded to the devil to sin, and on this account justly incurred the penalty of death; so, in his weakness and mortality, which he had brought upon himself, he should conquer the devil by the pain of death, while wholly avoiding sin. But this cannot be done, so long as from the deadly effect of the first transgression, man is conceived and born in sin.

Boso. Again I say that the thing is impossible, and reason approves what you say.

Anselm. Let me mention one thing more, without which man's reconciliation cannot be justly effected, and the impossibility is the same.

Boso. You have already presented so many obligations which we ought to fulfil, that nothing which you can add will alarm me more.

Anselm. Yet listen.

Boso. I will.

Chapter XXIII

What man took from God by his sin, which he has no power to repay.

Anselm. What did man take from God, when he allowed himself to be overcome by the devil?

Boso. Go on to mention, as you have begun, the evil things which can be added to those already shown for I am ignorant of them.

Anselm. Did not man take from God whatever He had purposed to do for human nature?

Boso. There is no denying that.

Anselm. Listen to the voice of strict justice; and judge according to that whether man makes to God a real satisfaction for his sin, unless, by overcoming the devil, man restore to God what he took from God in allowing himself to be conquered by the devil; so that, as by this conquest over man the devil took what belonged to God, and God was the loser, so in man's victory the devil may be despoiled, and God recover his right.

Boso. Surely nothing can be more exactly or justly conceived.

Anselm. Think you that supreme justice can violate this justice?

Boso. I dare not think it.

Anselm. Therefore man cannot and ought not by any means to receive from God what God designed to give him, unless he return to God everything which he took from him; so that, as by man God suffered loss, by man, also, He might recover His loss. But this cannot be effected except in this way: that, as in the fall of man all human nature was corrupted, and, as it were, tainted with sin, and God will not choose one of such a race to fill up the number in his heavenly kingdom; so, by man's victory, as many men may be justified from sin as are needed to complete the number which man was made to fill. But a sinful man can by no means do this, for a sinner cannot justify a sinner.

Boso. There is nothing more just or necessary; but, from all these things, the compassion of God and the hope of man seems to fail, as far as regards that happiness for which man was made.

Anselm. Yet wait a little.

Boso. Have you anything further?

CHAPTER XXIV

How, as long as man does not restore what he owes God, he cannot be happy, nor is he excused by want of power.

Anselm. If a man is called unjust who does not pay his fellow-man a debt, much more is he unjust who does not restore what he owes God.

Boso. If he can pay and yet does not, he is certainly unjust. But if he be not able, wherein is he unjust?

Anselm. Indeed, if the origin of his inability were not in himself, there might be some excuse for him. But if in this very impotence lies the fault, as it does not lessen the sin, neither does it excuse him from paying what is due. Suppose one should assign his slave a certain piece of work, and should command him not to throw himself into a ditch, which he points out to him and from which he could not extricate himself; and suppose that the slave, despising his master's command and warning, throws himself into the ditch before pointed out, so as to be utterly unable to accomplish the work assigned;

think you that his inability will at all excuse him for not doing his appointed work?

Boso. By no means, but will rather increase his crime, since he brought his inability upon himself. For doubly hath he sinned, in not doing what he was commanded to do and in doing what he was forewarned not to do.

Anselm. Just so inexcusable is man, who has voluntarily brought upon himself a debt which he cannot pay, and by his own fault disabled himself, so that he can neither escape his previous obligation not to sin, nor pay the debt which be has incurred by sin. For his very inability is guilt, because he ought not to have it; nay, he ought to be free from it; for as it is a crime not to have what he ought, it is also a crime to have what he ought not. Therefore, as it is a crime in man not to have that power which he received to avoid sin, it is also a crime to have that inability by which he can neither do right and avoid sin, nor restore the debt which he owes on account of his sin. For it is by his own free action that he loses that power, and falls into this inability. For not to have the power which one ought to have, is the same thing as to have the inability which one ought not to have. Therefore man's inability to restore what he owes to God, an inability brought upon himself for that very purpose, does not excuse man from paying; for the result of sin cannot excuse the sin itself.

Boso. This argument is exceedingly weighty, and must be true.

Anselm. Man, then, is unjust in not paying what he owes to God.

Boso. This is very true; for he is unjust, both in not paying, and in not being able to pay.

Anselm. But no unjust person shall be admitted to happiness; for as that happiness is complete in which there is nothing wanting, so it can belong to no one who is not so pure as to have no injustice found in him.

Boso. I dare not think otherwise.

Anselm. He, then, who does not pay God what he owes can never be happy.

Boso. I cannot deny that this is so.

Anselm. But if you choose to say that a merciful God remits to the suppliant his debt, because he cannot pay; God must be said to dispense with one of two things, viz., either this which man ought voluntarily to render but cannot, that is, an equivalent for his sin, a thing which ought not to be given up even to save the whole universe besides God; or else this, which, as I have before said, God was about to take away from man by punishment, even against man's will, viz., happiness. But if God gives up what man ought freely to render, for the reason that man cannot repay it, what is this but saying that God gives up what he is unable to obtain? But it is mockery to ascribe such compassion to God. But if God gives up what he was about to take from unwilling man, because man is unable to restore what he ought to restore freely, He abates the punishment and makes man happy on account of his sin, because he has what he ought not to have. For he ought not to have this inability, and therefore as long as he has it without atonement it is his sin. And truly such compassion on the part of God is wholly contrary to the Divine justice, which allows nothing but punishment as the recompense of sin. Therefore, as God cannot be inconsistent with himself, his compassion cannot be of this nature.

Boso. I think, then, we must look for another mercy than this.

Anselm. But suppose it were true that God pardons the man who does not pay his debt because he cannot.

Boso. I could wish it were so.

Anselm. But while man does not make payment, he either wishes to restore, or else he does not wish to. Now, if he wishes to do what he cannot, he will be needy, and if he does not wish to, he will be unjust.

Boso. Nothing can be plainer.

Anselm. But whether needy or unjust, he will not be happy.

Boso. This also is plain.

Anselm. So long, then, as he does not restore, he will not be happy.

Boso. If God follows the method of justice, there is no escape for the miserable wretch, and God's compassion seems to fail.

Anselm. You have demanded an explanation; now hear it. I do not deny that God is merciful, who preserveth man and beast, according to the multitude of his mercies. But we are speaking of that exceeding pity by which he makes man happy after this life. And I think that I have amply proved, by the reasons given above, that happiness ought not to be bestowed upon any one whose sins have not been wholly put away; and that this remission ought not to take place, save by the payment of the debt incurred by sin, according to the extent of sin. And if you think that any objections can be brought against these proofs, you ought to mention them.

Boso. I see not how your reasons can be at all invalidated.

Anselm. Nor do I, if rightly understood. But even if one of the whole number be confirmed by impregnable truth, that should be sufficient. For truth is equally secured against all doubt, if it be demonstrably proved by one argument as by many.

Boso. Surely this is so. But how, then, shall man be saved, if he neither pays what he owes, and ought not to be saved without paying? Or, with what face shall we declare that God, who is rich in mercy above human conception, cannot exercise this compassion?

Anselm. This is the question which you ought to ask of those in whose behalf you are speaking, who have no faith in the need of Christ for man's salvation, and you should also request them to tell how man can be saved without Christ. But, if they are utterly unable to do it, let them cease from mocking us, and let them hasten to unite themselves with us, who do not doubt that man can be saved through Christ; else let them despair of being saved at all. And if this terrifies them, let them believe in Christ as we do, that they may be saved.

Boso. Let me ask you, as I have begun, to show me how a man is saved by Christ.

Chapter XXV

How man's salvation by Christ is necessarily possible.

Anselm. Is it not sufficiently proved that man can be saved by Christ, when even infidels do not deny that man can be happy somehow, and it has been sufficiently shown that, leaving Christ out of view, no salvation can be found for man? For, either by Christ or by some one else can man be saved, or else not at all. If, then, it is false that man cannot be saved all, or that he can be saved in any other way, his salvation must necessarily be by Christ.

Boso. But what reply will you make to a person who perceives that man cannot be saved in any other way, and yet, not understanding how he can be saved by Christ, sees fit to declare that there cannot be any salvation either by Christ or in any other way?

Anselm. What reply ought to be made to one who ascribes impossibility to a necessary truth, because he does not understand how it can be?

Boso. That he is a fool.

Anselm. Then what he says must be despised.

Boso. Very true; but we ought to show him in what way the thing is true which he holds to be impossible.

Anselm. Do you not perceive, from what we have said above, that it is necessary for some men to attain to felicity? For, if it is unfitting for God to elevate man with any stain upon him, to that for which he made him free from all stain, lest it should seem that God had repented of his good intent, or was unable to accomplish his designs; far more is it impossible, on account of the same unfitness, that no man should be exalted to that state for which he was made. Therefore, a satisfaction such as we have above proved necessary for sin, must be found apart from the Christian faith, which no reason can show; or else we must accept the Christian doctrine. For what is clearly made out by absolute reasoning ought by no means to be questioned, even though the method of it be not understood.

Boso. What you say is true.

Anselm. Why, then, do you question further?

Boso. I come not for this purpose, to have you remove doubts from my faith, but to have you show me the reason for my confidence. Therefore, as you have brought me thus far by your reasoning, so that I perceive that man as a sinner owes God for his sin what he is unable to pay, and cannot be saved without paying; I wish you would go further with me, and enable me to understand, by force of reasoning, the fitness of all those things which the Catholic faith enjoins upon us with regard to Christ, if we hope to be saved; and how they avail for the salvation of man, and how God saves man by compassion; when he never remits his sin, unless man shall have rendered what was due on account of his sin. And, to make your reasoning the clearer, begin at the beginning, so as to rest it upon a strong foundation.

Anselm. Now God help me, for you do not spare me in the least, nor consider the weakness of my skill, when you enjoin so great a work upon me. Yet I will attempt it, as I have begun, not trusting in myself but in God, and will do what I can with his help. But let us separate the things which remain to be said from those which have been said, by a new introduction, lest by their unbroken length, these things become tedious to one who wishes to read them.

Book Second

Chapter I

How man was made holy by God, so as to be happy in the enjoyment of God.

Anselm. It ought not to be disputed that rational nature was made holy by God, in order to be happy in enjoying Him. For to this end is it rational, in order to discern justice and injustice, good and evil, and between the greater and the lesser good. Otherwise it was made rational in vain. But God made it not rational in vain. Wherefore, doubtless, it was made rational for this end. In like manner is it proved that the intelligent creature received the power of discernment for this purpose, that he might hate and shun evil, and love and choose good, and especially the greater good. For else in vain would God have given him that power of discernment, since man's discretion would be useless unless he loved and avoided according to it. But it does not befit God to give such power in vain. It is, therefore, established that rational nature was created for this end, viz., to love and choose the highest good supremely, for its own sake and nothing else; for if the highest good were chosen for any other reason, then something else and not itself would be the thing loved. But intelligent nature cannot fulfil this purpose without being holy. Therefore that it might not in vain be made rational, it was made, in order to fulfil this purpose, both rational and holy. Now, if it was made holy in order to choose and love the highest good, then it was made such in order to follow sometimes what it loved and chose, or else it was not. But if it were not made holy for this end, that it might follow what it loves and chooses, then in vain was it made to love and choose holiness; and there can be no reason why it should be ever bound to follow holiness. Therefore, as long as it will be holy in loving and choosing the supreme good, for which it was made, it will be miserable; because it will be impotent despite of its will, inasmuch as it does not have what it desires. But this is utterly absurd. Wherefore rational nature was made holy, in order to be happy in enjoying the supreme good, which is God. Therefore man, whose nature is rational, was made holy for this end, that he might be happy in enjoying God.

CHAPTER II

How man would never have died, unless he had sinned.

Anselm. Moreover, it is easily proved that man was so made as not to be necessarily subject to death; for, as we have already said, it is inconsistent with God's wisdom and justice to compel man to suffer death without fault, when he made him holy to enjoy eternal blessedness. It therefore follows that had man never sinned he never would have died.

Chapter III

How man will rise with the same body which he has in this world.

Anselm. From this the future resurrection of the dead is clearly proved. For if man is to be perfectly restored, the restoration should make him such as he would have been had he never sinned.

Boso. It must be so.

Anselm. Therefore, as man, had he not sinned, was to have been transferred with the same body to an immortal state, so when he shall be restored, it must properly be with his own body as he lived in this world.

Boso. But what shall we say to one who tells us that this is right enough with regard to those in whom humanity shall be perfectly restored, but is not necessary as respects the reprobate?

Anselm. We know of nothing more just or proper than this, that as man, had he continued in holiness, would have been perfectly happy for eternity, both in body and in soul; so, if he persevere in wickedness, he shall be likewise completely miserable forever.

Boso. You have promptly satisfied me in these matters.

Chapter IV

How God will complete, in respect to human nature, what he has begun.

Anselm. From these things, we can easily see that God will either complete what he has begun with regard to human nature, or else he has made to no end so lofty a nature, capable of so great good. Now if it be understood that God has made nothing more valuable than rational existence capable of enjoying him; it is altogether foreign from his character to suppose that he will suffer that rational existence utterly to perish.

Boso. No reasonable being can think otherwise.

Anselm. Therefore is it necessary for him to perfect in human nature what he has begun. But this, as we have already said, cannot be accomplished save by a complete expiation of sin, which no sinner can effect for himself.

Boso. I now understand it to be necessary for God to complete what he has begun, lest there be an unseemly falling off from his design.

Chapter V

How, although the thing may be necessary, God may not do it by a compulsory necessity; and what is the nature of that necessity which removes or lessens gratitude, and what necessity increases it.

Boso. But if it be so, then God seems as it were compelled, for the sake of avoiding what is unbecoming, to secure the salvation of man. How, then, can it be denied that he does it more on his own account than on ours? But if it be so, what thanks do we owe him for what he does for himself? How shall we attribute our salvation to his grace, if he saves us from necessity?

Anselm. There is a necessity which takes away or lessens our gratitude to a benefactor, and there is also a necessity by which the favor deserves still greater thanks. For when one does a benefit from a necessity to which he is unwillingly subjected, less thanks are due him, or none at all. But when he freely places himself under the necessity of benefiting another, and sustains that necessity without reluctance, then he certainly deserves greater thanks for the favor. For this should not be called necessity but grace, inasmuch as he undertook or maintains it, not with any constraint, but freely. For if that which to-day you promise of your own accord you will give to-morrow, you do give to-morrow with the same willingness; though it be necessary for you, if possible, to redeem your promise, or make yourself a liar; notwithstanding, the recipient of your favor is as much indebted for your precious gift as if you had not promised it, for you were not obliged to make yourself his debtor before the time of giving it: just so is it when one undertakes, by a vow, a design of holy living. For though after his vow he ought necessarily to perform, lest he suffer the judgment of an apostate, and, although he may be compelled to keep it even unwillingly, yet, if he keep his vow cheerfully, he is not less but more pleasing to God than if he had not vowed. For he has not only given up the life of the world, but also his personal liberty, for the sake of God; and he cannot be said to live a holy life of necessity, but with the same freedom with which he took the vow. Much more, therefore, do we owe all thanks to God for completing his intended favor to man; though, indeed, it would not be proper for him to fail in his good design, because wanting nothing in himself he begun it for our sake and not his own. For what man was about to do was not hidden from God at his creation; and yet by freely creating man, God as it were bound himself to complete the good which he had begun. In fine, God does nothing by necessity, since he is not compelled or restrained in anything. And when we say that God does anything to avoid dishonor, which he certainly does not fear, we must mean that God does this from the necessity of maintaining his honor; which necessity is after all no more than this, viz., the immutability of his honor, which belongs to him in himself, and is not derived from another; and therefore it is not properly called necessity. Yet we may say, although the whole work which God does for man is of grace, that it is necessary for God, on account of his unchangeable goodness, to complete the work which he has begun.

Boso. I grant it.

Chapter VI

How no being, except the God-man, can make the atonement by which man is saved.

Anselm. But this cannot be effected, except the price paid to God for the sin of man be something greater than all the universe besides God.

Boso. So it appears.

Anselm. Moreover, it is necessary that he who can give God anything of his own which is more valuable than all things in the possession of God, must be greater than all else but God himself.

Boso. I cannot deny it.

Anselm. Therefore none but God can make this satisfaction.

Boso. So it appears.

Anselm. But none but a man ought to do this, other wise man does not make the satisfaction.

Boso. Nothing seems more just.

Anselm. If it be necessary, therefore, as it appears, that the heavenly kingdom be made up of men, and this cannot be effected unless the aforesaid satisfaction be made, which none but God can make and none but man ought to make, it is necessary for the God-man to make it.

Boso. Now blessed be God! we have made a great discovery with regard to our question. Go on, therefore, as you have begun. For I hope that God will assist you.

Anselm. Now must we inquire how God can become man.

Chapter VII

How necessary it is for the same being to be perfect God and perfect man.

Anselm. The Divine and human natures cannot alternate, so that the Divine should become human or the human Divine; nor can they be so commingled as that a third should be produced from the two which is neither wholly Divine nor wholly human. For, granting that it were possible for either to be changed into the other, it would in that case be only God and not man, or man only and not God. Or, if they were so commingled that a third nature sprung from the combination of the two (as from two animals, a male and a female of different species, a third is produced, which does not preserve entire the species of either parent, but has a mixed nature derived from both), it would neither be God nor man. Therefore the God-man, whom we require to be of a nature both human and Divine, cannot be produced by a change from one into the other, nor by an imperfect commingling of both in a third; since these things cannot be, or, if they could be, would avail nothing to our purpose. Moreover, if these two complete natures are said to be joined somehow, in such a way that one may be Divine while the other is human, and yet that which is God not be the same with that which is man, it is impossible for both to do the work necessary to be accomplished. For God will not do it, because he has no debt to pay; and man will not do it, because he cannot. Therefore, in order that the God-man may perform this, it is necessary that the same being should perfect God and perfect man, in order to make this atonement. For he cannot and ought not to do it, unless he be very God and very man. Since, then, it is necessary that the God-man preserve the completeness of each nature, it is no less necessary that these two natures be united entire in one person, just as a body and a reasonable soul exist together in every human being; for otherwise it is impossible that the same being should be very God and very man.

Boso. All that you say is satisfactory to me.

Chapter VIII

How it behoved God to take a man of the race of Adam, and born of a woman.

Anselm. It now remains to inquire whence and how God shall assume human nature. For he will either take it from Adam, or else he will make a new man, as he made Adam originally. But, if he makes a new man, not of Adam's race, then this man will not belong to the human family, which descended from Adam, and therefore ought not to make atonement for it, because he never belonged to it. For, as it is right for man to make atonement for the sin of man, it is also necessary that he who makes the atonement should be the very being who has sinned, or else one of the same race. Otherwise, neither Adam nor his race would make satisfaction for themselves. Therefore, as through Adam and Eve sin was propagated among all men, so none but themselves, or one born of them, ought to make atonement for the sin of men. And, since they cannot, one born of them must fulfil this work. Moreover, as Adam and his whole race, had he not sinned, would have stood firm without the support of any other being, so, after the fall, the same race must rise and be exalted by means of itself. For, whoever restores the race to its place, it will certainly stand by that being who has made this restoration. Also, when God created human nature in Adam alone, and would only make woman out of man, that by the union of both sexes there might be increase, in this he showed plainly that he wished to produce all that he intended with regard to human nature from man alone. Wherefore, if the race of Adam be reinstated by any being not of the same race, it will not be restored to that dignity which it would have had, had not Adam sinned, and so will not be completely restored; and, besides, God will seem to have failed of his purpose, both which suppositions are incongruous: It is, therefore, necessary that the man by whom Adam's race shall be restored be taken from Adam.

Boso. If we follow reason, as we proposed to do, this is the necessary result.

Anselm. Let us now examine the question, whether the human nature taken by God must be produced from a father and mother, as other men are, or from man alone, or from woman alone. For, in whichever of these three modes it be, it will be produced from Adam and Eve, for from these two is every person of either sex descended. And of these three modes, no one is easier for God than another, that it should be selected on this account.

Boso. So far, it is well.

Anselm. It is no great toil to show that that man will be brought into existence in a nobler and purer manner, if produced from man alone, or woman alone, than if springing from the union of both, as do all other men.

Boso. I agree with you.

Anselm. Therefore must he be taken either from man alone, or woman alone.

Boso. There is no other source.

Anselm. In four ways can God create man, viz., either of man and woman, in the common way; or neither of man nor woman, as he created Adam; or of man without woman, as he made Eve; or of woman without man, which thus far he has never done. Wherefore, in order to show that this last mode also under his power, and was reserved for this very purpose, what more fitting than that he should take that man whose origin we are seeking from a woman without a man? Now whether it be more worthy that he be born of a virgin, or one not a virgin, we need not discuss, but must affirm, beyond all doubt, that the God-man should be born of a virgin.

Boso. Your speech gratifies my heart.

Anselm. Does what we have said appear sound, or is it unsubstantial as a cloud, as you have said infidels declare?

Boso. Nothing can be more sound.

Anselm. Paint not, therefore, upon baseless emptiness, but upon solid truth, and tell how clearly fitting it is that, as man's sin and the cause of our condemnation sprung from a woman, so the cure of sin and the source of our salvation should also be found in a woman. And that women may not despair of attaining the inheritance of the blessed, because that so dire an evil arose from woman, it is proper that from woman also so great a blessing should arise, that their hopes may be revived. Take also this view. If it was a virgin which brought all evil upon the race, it is much more appropriate that a virgin should be the occasion of all good. And this also. If woman, whom God made from man alone, was made of a virgin (*de virgine*), it is peculiarly fitting for that man also, who shall spring from a woman, to be born of a woman without man. Of the pictures which can be superadded to this, showing that the God-man ought to be born of a virgin, we will say nothing. These are sufficient.

Boso. They are certainly very beautiful and reasonable.

Chapter IX

How of necessity the Word only can unite in one person with man.

Anselm. Now must we inquire further, in what person God, who exists in three persons, shall take upon himself the nature of man. For a plurality of persons cannot take one and the same man into a unity of person. Wherefore in one person only can this be done. But, as respects this personal unity of God and man, and in which of the Divine persons this ought to be effected, I have expressed myself, as far as I think needful for the present inquiry, in a letter on the Incarnation of the Word, addressed to my lord, the Pope Urban.

Boso. Yet briefly glance at this matter, why the person of the Son should be incarnated rather than that of the Father or the Holy Spirit.

Anselm. If one of the other persons be incarnated, there will be two sons in the Trinity, viz., the Son of

God, who is the Son before the incarnation, and he also who, by the incarnation, will be the son of the virgin; and among the persons which ought always to be equal there will be an inequality as respects the dignity of birth. For the one born of God will have a nobler birth than he who is born of the virgin. Likewise, if the Father become incarnate, there will be two grandsons in the Trinity; for the Father, by assuming humanity, will be the grandson of the parents of the virgin, and the Word, though having nothing to do with man, will yet be the grandson of the virgin, since he will be the son of her son. But all these things are incongruous and do not pertain to the incarnation of the Word. And there is yet another reason which renders it more fitting for the Son to become incarnate than the other persons. It is, that for the Son to pray to the Father is more proper than for any other person of the Trinity to supplicate his fellow. Moreover, man, for whom he was to pray, and the devil, whom he was to vanquish, have both put on a false likeness to God by their own will. Wherefore they have sinned, as it were, especially against the person of the Son, who is believed to be the very image of God. Wherefore the punishment or pardon of guilt is with peculiar propriety ascribed to him upon whom chiefly the injury was inflicted. Since, therefore, infallible reason has brought us to this necessary conclusion, that the Divine and human natures must unite in one person, and that this is evidently more fitting in respect to the person of the Word than the other persons, we determine that God the Word must unite with man in one person.

Boso. The way by which you lead me is so guarded by reason that I cannot deviate from it to the right or left.

Anselm. It is not I who lead you, but he of whom we are speaking, without whose guidance we have no power to keep the way of truth.

CHAPTER X

How this man dies not of debt; and in what sense he can or cannot sin; and how neither he nor an angel deserves praise for their holiness, if it is impossible for them to sin.

Anselm. We ought not to question whether this man was about to die as a debt, as all other men do. For, if Adam would not have died had he not committed sin, much less should this man suffer death, in whom there can be no sin, for he is God.

Boso. Let me delay you a little on this point. For in either case it is no slight question with me whether it be said that he can sin or that he cannot. For if it be said that he cannot sin, it should seem hard to be believed. For to say a word concerning him, not as of one who never existed in the manner we have spoken hitherto, but as of one whom we know and whose deeds we know; who, I say, will deny that he could have done many things which we call sinful? For, to say nothing of other things, how shall we say that it was not possible for him to commit the sin of lying? For, when he says to the Jews, of his Father: "If I say that I know him not, I shall be a liar, like unto you," and, in this sentence, makes use of the words: "I know him not," who says that he could not have uttered these same four words, or expressing the same thing differently, have declared, "I know him not?" Now had he done so, he would have been a liar, as he himself says, and therefore a sinner. Therefore, since he could do this, he could sin.

Anselm. It is true that he could say this, and also that he could not sin.

Boso. How is that?

Anselm. All power follows the will. For, when I say that I can speak or walk, it is understood, if I choose. For, if the will be not implied as acting, there is no power, but only necessity. For, when I say that I can be dragged or bound unwillingly, this is not my power, but necessity and the power of another; since I am able to be dragged or bound in no other sense than this, that another can drag or bind me. So we can say of Christ, that he could lie, so long as we understand, if he chose to do so. And, since he could not lie unwillingly and could not wish to lie, none the less can it be said that he could not lie.

So in this way it is both true that he could and could not lie.

Boso. Now let us return to our original inquiry with regard to that man, as if nothing were known of him. I say, then, if he were unable to sin, because, according to you, he could not wish to sin, he maintains holiness of necessity, and therefore he will not be holy from free will. What thanks, then, will he deserve for his holiness? For we are accustomed to say that God made man and angel capable of sinning on this account, that, when of their own free will they maintained holiness, though they might have abandoned it, they might deserve commendation and reward, which they would not have done had they been necessarily holy.

Anselm. Are not the angels worthy of praise, though unable to commit sin?

Boso. Doubtless they are, because they deserved this present inability to sin from the fact that when they could sin they refused to do so.

Anselm. What say you with respect to God, who cannot sin, and yet has not deserved this, by refusing to sin when he had the power? Must not he be praised for his holiness?

Boso. I should like to have you answer that question for me; for if I say that he deserves no praise, I know that I speak falsely. If, on the other hand, I say that he does deserve praise, I am afraid of invalidating my reasoning with respect to the angels.

Anselm. The angels are not to be praised for their holiness because they could sin, but because it is owing to themselves, in a certain sense, that now they cannot sin. And in this respect are they in a measure like God, who has, from himself, whatever he possesses. For a person is said to give a thing, who does not take it away when he can; and to do a thing is but the same as not to prevent it, when that is in one's power. When, therefore, the angel could depart from holiness and yet did not, and could make himself unholy yet did not, we say with propriety that he conferred virtue upon himself and made himself holy. In this sense, therefore, has he holiness of himself (for the creature cannot have it of himself in any other way), and, therefore, should be praised for his holiness, because he is not holy of necessity but freely; for that is improperly called necessity which involves neither compulsion nor restraint. Wherefore, since whatever God has he has perfectly of himself, he is most of all to be praised for the good things which he possesses and maintains not by any necessity, but, as before said, by his own infinite unchangeableness. Therefore, likewise, that man who will be also God since every good thing which he possesses comes from himself, will be holy not of necessity but voluntarily, and, therefore, will deserve praise. For, though human nature will have what it has from the Divine nature, yet it will likewise have it from itself, since the two natures will be united in one person.

Boso. You have satisfied me on this point; and I see clearly that it is both true that he could not sin, and yet that he deserves praise for his holiness. But now I think the question arises, since God could make such a man, why he did not create angels and our first parents so as to be incapable of sin, and yet praiseworthy for their holiness?

Anselm. Do you know what you are saying?

Boso. I think I understand, and it is therefore I ask why he did not make them so.

Anselm. Because it was neither possible nor right for any one of them to be the same with God, as we say that man was. And if you ask why he did not bring the three persons, or at least the Word, into unity with men at that time, I answer: Because reason did not at all demand any such thing then, but wholly forbade it, for God does nothing without reason.

Boso. I blush to have asked the question. Go on with what you have to say.

Anselm. We must conclude, then, that he should not be subject to death, inasmuch as he will not be a sinner.

Boso. I must agree with you.

Chapter XI

How Christ dies of his own power, and how mortality does not inhere in the essential nature of man.

Anselm. Now, also, it remains to inquire whether, as man's nature is, it is possible for that man to die?

Boso. We need hardly dispute with regard to this, since he will be really man, and every man is by nature mortal.

Anselm. I do not think mortality inheres in the essential nature of man, but only as corrupted. Since, had man never sinned, and had his immortality been unchangeably confirmed, he would have been as really man; and, when the dying rise again, incorruptible, they will no less be really men. For, if mortality was an essential attribute of human nature, then he who was immortal could not be man. Wherefore, neither corruption nor incorruption belong essentially to human nature, for neither makes nor destroys a man; but happiness accrues to him from the one, and misery from the other. But since all men die, mortality is included in the definition of man, as given by philosophers, for they have never even believed in the possibility of man's being immortal in all respects. And so it is not enough to prove that that man ought to be subject to death, for us to say that he will be in all respects a man.

Boso. Seek then for some other reason, since I know of none, if you do not, by which we may prove that he can die.

Anselm. We may not doubt that, as he will be God, he will possess omnipotence.

Boso. Certainly.

Anselm. He can, then, if he chooses, lay down his life and take it again.

Boso. If not, he would scarcely seem to be omnipotent.

Anselm. Therefore is he able to avoid death if he chooses, and also to die and rise again. Moreover, whether he lays down his life by the intervention of no other person, or another causes this, so that he lays it down by permitting it to be taken, it makes no difference as far as regards his power.

Boso. There is no doubt about it.

Anselm. If, then, he chooses to allow it, he could be slain; and if he were unwilling to allow it, he couId not be slain.

Boso. To this we are unavoidably brought by reason.

Anselin. Reason has also taught us that the gift which he presents to God, not of debt but freely, ought to be something greater than anything in the possession of God.

Boso. Yes.

Anselin. Now this can neither be found beneath him nor above him.

Boso. Very true.

Anselm. In himself, therefore, must it be found.

Boso. So it appears.

Anselm. Therefore will he give himself, or something pertaining to himself.

Boso. I cannot see how it should be otherwise.

Anselm. Now must we inquire what sort of a gift this should be? For he may not give himself to God, or anything of his, as if God did not have what was his own. For every creature belongs to God.

Boso. This is so.

Anselm. Therefore must this gift be understood in this way, that he somehow gives up himself, or something of his, to the honor of God, which he did not owe as a debtor.

Boso. So it seems from what has been already said.

Anselm. If we say that he will give himself to God by obedience, so as, by steadily maintaining holiness, to render himself subject to his will, this will not be giving a thing not demanded of him by God as his due. For every reasonable being owes his obedience to God.

Boso. This cannot be denied.

Anselm. Therefore must it be in some other way that he gives himself, or something belonging to him, to God.

Boso. Reason urges us to this conclusion.

Anslem. Let us see whether, perchance, this may be to give up his life or to lay down his life, or to deliver himself up to death for God's honor. For God will not demand this of him as a debt; for, as no sin will be found, he ought not to die, as we have already said.

Boso. Else I cannot understand it.

Anselm. But let us further observe whether this is according to reason.

Boso. Speak you, and I will listen with pleasure.

Anselm. If man sinned with ease, is it not fitting for him to atone with difficulty? And if he was overcome by the devil in the easiest manner possible, so as to dishonor God by sinning against him, is it not right that man, in making satisfaction for his sin, should honor God by conquering the devil with the greatest possible difficulty? Is it not proper that, since man has departed from God as far as possible in his sin, he should make to God the greatest possible satisfaction?

Boso. Surely, there is nothing more reasonable.

Anselm. Now, nothing can be more severe or difficult for man to do for God's honor, than to suffer death voluntarily when not bound by obligation; and man cannot give himself to God in any way more truly than by surrendering himself to death for God's honor.

Boso. All these things are true.

Anselm. Therefore, he who wishes to make atonement for man's sin should be one who can die if he chooses.

Boso. I think it is plain that the man whom we seek for should not only be one who is not necessarily subject to death on account of his omnipotence, and one who does not deserve death on account of his sin, but also one who can die of his own free will, for this will be necessary.

Anselm. There are also many other reasons why it is peculiarly fitting for that man to enter into the common intercourse of men, and maintain a likeness to them, only without sin. And these things are more easily and clearly manifest in his life and actions than they can possibly be shown to be by mere reason without experience. For who can say how necessary and wise a thing it was for him who was to redeem mankind, and lead them back by his teaching from the way of death and destruction into the path of life and eternal happiness, when he conversed with men, and when he taught them by personal intercourse, to set them an example himself of the way in which they ought to live? But how could he have given this example to weak and dying men, that they should not deviate from holiness because of injuries, or scorn, or tortures, or even death, had they not been able to recognise all these virtues in himself?

CHAPTER XII

How, though he share in our weakness, he is not therefore miserable.

Boso. All these things plainly show that he ought to be mortal and to partake of our weaknesses. But all these things are our miseries. Will he then be miserable?

Anselm. No, indeed! For as no advantage which one has apart from his choice constitutes happiness, so there is no misery in choosing to bear a loss, when the choice is a wise one and made without compulsion.

Boso. Certainly, this must be allowed.

Chapter XIII

How, along with our other weaknesses, he does not partake of our ignorance.

Boso. But tell me whether, in this likeness to men which he ought to have, he will inherit also our ignorance, as he does our other infirmities?

Anselm. Do you doubt the omnipotence of God?

Boso. No! but, although this man be immortal in respect to his Divine nature, yet will he be mortal in his human nature. For why will he not be like them in their ignorance, as he is in their mortality?

Anselm. That union of humanity with the Divine person will not be effected except in accordance with the highest wisdom; and, therefore, God will not take anything belonging to man which is only useless, but even a hindrance to the work which that man must accomplish. For ignorance is in no respect useful, but very prejudicial. How can he perform works, so many and so great, without the highest wisdom? Or, how will men believe him if they find him ignorant? And if he be ignorant, what will it avail him? If nothing is loved except as it is known, and there be no good thing which he does not love, then there can be no good thing of which be is ignorant. But no one perfectly understands good, save he who can distinguish it from evil; and no one can make this distinction who does not know what evil is. Therefore, as he of whom we are speaking perfectly comprehends what is good, so there can be no evil with which he is unacquainted. Therefore must he have all knowledge, though he do not openly show it in his intercourse with men.

Boso. In his more mature years, this should seem to he as you say; but, in infancy, as it will not be a fit time to discover wisdom, so there will be no need, and therefore no propriety, in his having it.

Anselm. Did not I say that the incarnation will be made in wisdom? But God will in wisdom assume that mortality, which he makes use of so widely, because for so great an object. But he could not wisely assume ignorance, for this is never useful, but always injurious, except when an evil will is deterred from acting, on account of it. But, in him an evil desire never existed. For if ignorance did no harm in any other respect, yet does it in this, that it takes away the good of knowing. And to answer your question in a word: that man, from the essential nature of his being, will be always full of God; and, therefore, will never want the power, the firmness or the wisdom of God.

Boso. Though wholly unable to doubt the truth of this with respect to Christ, yet, on this very account, have I asked for the reason of it. For we are often certain about a thing, and yet cannot prove it by reason.

Chapter XIV

How his death outweighs the number and greatness of our sins.

Boso. Now I ask you to tell me how his death can outweigh the number and magnitude of our sins, when the least sin we can think of you have shown to be so monstrous that, were there an infinite number of worlds as full of created existence as this, they could not stand, but would fall back into nothing, sooner than one look should be made contrary to the just will of God.

Anselm. Were that man here before you, and you knew who he was, and it were told you that, if you did not kill him, the whole universe, except God, would perish, would you do it to preserve the rest of creation?

Boso. No! not even were an infinite number of worlds displayed before me.

Anselm. But suppose you were told: "If you do not kill him, all the sins of the world will be heaped upon you."

Boso. I should answer, that I would far rather bear all other sins, not only those of this world, past and future, but also all others that can be conceived of, than this alone. And I think I ought to say this, not only with regard to killing him, but even as to the slightest injury which could be inflicted on him.

Anselm. You judge correctly; but tell me why it is that your heart recoils from one injury inflicted upon him as more heinous than all other sins that can be thought of, inasmuch as all sins whatsoever are committed against him?

Boso. A sin committed upon his person exceeds beyond comparison all the sins which can be thought of, that do not affect his person.

Anselm. What say you to this, that one often suffers freely certain evils in his person, in order not to suffer greater ones in his property?

Boso. God has no need of such patience, for all things lie in subjection to his power, as you answered a certain question of mine above.

Anselm. You say well; and hence we see that no enormity or multitude of sins, apart from the Divine person, can for a moment be compared with a bodily injury inflicted upon that man.

Boso. This is most plain.

Anselm. How great does this good seem to you, if the destruction of it is such an evil?

Boso. If its existence is as great a good as its destruction is an evil, then is it far more a good than those sins are evils which its destruction so far surpasses.

Anselm. Very true. Consider, also, that sins are as hateful as they are evil, and that life is only amiable in proportion as it is good. And, therefore, it follows that that life is more lovely than sins are odious.

Boso. I cannot help seeing this.

Anselm. And do you not think that so great a good in itself so lovely, can avail to pay what is due for the sins of the whole world?

Boso. Yes! it has even infinite value.

Anselm. Do you see, then, how this life conquers all sins, if it be given for them?

Boso. Plainly.

Anselm. If, then, to lay down life is the same as to suffer death, as the gift of his life surpasses all the sins of men, so will also the suffering of death.

Chapter XV

How this death removes even the sins of his murderers.

Boso. This is properly so with regard to all sins not affecting the person of the Deity. But let me ask you one thing more. If it be as great an evil to slay him as his life is a good, how can his death overcome and destroy the sins of those who slew him? Or, if it destroys the sin of any one of them, how can it not also destroy any sin committed by other men? For we believe that many men will be saved, and a vast many will not be saved.

Anselm. The Apostle answers the question when he says: "Had they known it, they would never have crucified the Lord of glory." For a sin knowingly committed and a sin done ignorantly are so different that an evil which they could never do, were its full extent known, may be pardonable when done in ignorance. For no man could ever, knowingly at least, slay the Lord; and, therefore, those who did it in ignorance did not rush into that transcendental crime with which none others can be compared. For this crime, the magnitude of which we have been considering as equal to the worth of his life, we have not looked at as having been ignorantly done, but knowingly; a thing which no man ever did or could do.

Boso. You have reasonably shown that the murderers of Christ can obtain pardon for their sin.

Anselm. What more do you ask? For now you, see how reason of necessity shows that the celestial state must be made up from men, and that this can only be by the forgiveness of sins, which man can never have but by man, who must be at the same time Divine, and reconcile sinners to God by his own death. Therefore have we clearly found that Christ, whom we confess to be both God and man, died for us; and, when this is known beyond all doubt, all things which he says of himself must be acknowledged as true, for God cannot lie, and all he does must be received as wisely done, though we do not understand the reason of it.

Boso. What you say is true; and I do not for a moment doubt that his words are true, and all that he does reasonable. But I ask this in order that you may disclose to me, in their true rationality, those things in Christian faith which seem to infidels improper or impossible; and this, not to strengthen me in the faith, but to gratify one already confirmed by the knowledge of the truth itself.

Chapter XVI

How God took that man from a sinful substance, and yet without sin; and of the salvation of Adam and Eve.

Boso. As, therefore, you have disclosed the reason of those things mentioned above, I beg you will also explain what I am now about to ask. First, then, how does God, from a sinful substance, that is, of human species, which was wholly tainted by sin, take, a man without sin, as an unleavened lump from that which is leavened? For, though the conception of this man be pure, and free from the sin of fleshly gratification, yet the virgin herself, from whom he sprang, was conceived in iniquity, and in sin did her mother bear her, since she herself sinned in Adam, in whom all men sinned.

Anselm. Since it is fitting for that man to be God, and also the restorer of sinners, we doubt not that he is wholly without sin; yet will this avail nothing, unless he be taken without sin and yet of a sinful substance. But if we cannot comprehend in what manner the wisdom of God effects this, we should be surprised, but with reverence should allow of a thing of so great magnitude to remain hidden from us. For the restoring of human nature by God is more wonderful than its creation; for either was equally easy for God; but before man was made he had not sinned so that he ought not to be denied existence. But after man was made he deserved, by his sin, to lose his existence together with its design; though he never has wholly lost this, viz., that he should be one capable of being punished, or of receiving God's compassion. For neither of these things could take effect if he were annihilated. Therefore God's restoring man is more wonderful than his creating man, inasmuch as it is done for the sinner contrary to his deserts; while the act of creation was not for the sinner, and was not in opposition to man's deserts. How great a thing it is, also, for God and man to unite in one person, that, while the perfection of each nature is preserved, the same being may be both God and man! Who, then, will dare to think that the human mind can discover how wisely, how wonderfully, so incomprehensible a work has been accomplished?

Boso. I allow that no man can wholly discover so great a mystery in this life, and I do not desire you to do what no man can do, but only to explain it according to your ability. For you will sooner convince me that deeper reasons lie concealed in this matter, by showing some one that you know of, than if, by saying nothing, you make it appear that you do not understand any reason.

Anselm. I see that I cannot escape your importunity; but if I have any power to explain what you wish, let us thank God for it. But if not, let the things above said suffice. For, since it is agreed that God ought to become man, no doubt He will not lack the wisdom or the power to effect this without sin.

Boso. This I readily allow.

Anselm. It was certainly proper that that atonement which Christ made should benefit not only those who lived at that time but also others. For, suppose there were a king against whom all the people of his provinces had rebelled, with but a single exception of those belonging to their race, and that all the rest were irretrievably under condemnation. And suppose that he who alone is blameless had so great favor with the king, and so deep love for us, as to be both able and willing to save all those who trusted in his guidance; and this because of a certain very pleasing service which he was about to do for the king, according to his desire; and, inasmuch as those who are to be pardoned cannot all assemble upon that day, the king grants, on account of the greatness of the service performed, that whoever, either before or after the day appointed, acknowledged that he wished to obtain pardon by the work that day accomplished, and to subscribe to the condition there laid down, should be freed from all past guilt; and, if they sinned after this pardon, and yet wished to render atonement and to be set right again by the efficacy of this plan, they should again be pardoned, only provided that no one enter his mansion until this thing be accomplished by which his sins are removed. In like manner, since all who are to be saved cannot be present at the sacrifice of Christ, yet such virtue is there in his death that its power is extended even to those far remote in place or time. But that it ought to benefit not merely those present is plainly evident, because there could not be so many living at the time of his death as are necessary to complete the heavenly state, even if all who were upon the earth at that time were admitted to the benefits of redemption. For the number of evil angels which must be made up from men is greater than the number of men at that time living. Nor may we believe that, since man was created, there was ever a time when the world, with the creatures made for the use of man, was so unprofitable as to contain no human being who had gained the object for which he was made. For it seems unfitting that God should even for a moment allow the human race, made to complete the heavenly state, and those creatures which he made for their use, to exist in vain.

Boso. You show by correct reasoning, such as nothing can oppose, that there never was a time since man was created when there has not been some one who was gaining that reconciliation without which every man was made in vain. So that we rest upon this as not only proper but also necessary. For if this is more fit and reasonable than that at any time there should be no one found fulfilling the design for which God made man, and there is no further objection that can be made to this view, then it is necessary that there always be some person partaking of this promised pardon. And, therefore, we must not doubt that Adam and Eve obtained part in that forgiveness, though Divine authority makes no mention of this.

Anselm. It is also incredible that God created them, and unchangeably determined to make all men from them, as many as were needed for the celestial state, and yet should exclude these two from this design.

Boso. Nay, undoubtedly we ought to believe that God made them for this purpose, viz., to belong to the number of those for whose sake they were created.

Anselm. You understand it well. But no soul, before the death of Christ, could enter the heavenly kingdom, as I said above, with regard to the palace of the king.

Boso. So we believe.

Anselm. Moreover, the virgin, from whom that man was taken of whom we are speaking, was of the number of those who were cleansed from their sins before his birth, and he was born of her in her purity.

Boso. What you say would satisfy me, were it not that he ought to be pure of himself, whereas he appears to have his purity from his mother and not from himself.

Anselm. Not so. But as the mother's purity, which he partakes, was only derived from him, he also was pure by and of himself.

Chapter XVII

How he did not die of necessity, though he could not be born, except as destined to suffer death.

Boso. Thus far it is well. But there is yet another matter that needs to be looked into. For we have said before that his death was not to be a matter of necessity; yet now we see that his mother was purified by the power of his death, when without this he could not have been born of her. How, then, was not his death necessary, when he could not have been, except in view of future death? For if he were not to die, the virgin of whom he was born could not be pure, since this could only be effected by true faith in his death, and, if she were not pure, he could not be born of her. If, therefore, his death be not a necessary consequence of his being born of the virgin, he never could have been born of her at all; but this is an absurdity.

Anselm. If you had carefully noted the remarks made above, you would easily have discovered in them, I think, the answer to your question.

Boso. I see not how.

Anselm. Did we not find, when considering the question whether he would lie, that there were two senses of the word *power* in regard to it, the one referring to his disposition, the other to the act itself; and that, though having the power to lie, he was so constituted by nature as not to wish to lie, and, therefore, deserved praise for his holiness in maintaining the truth?

Boso. It is so.

Anselm. In like manner, with regard to the preservation of his life, there is the power of preserving and the power of wishing to preserve it. And when the question is asked whether the same God-man could preserve his life, so as never to die, we must not doubt that he always had the power to preserve his life, though he could not wish to do so for the purpose of escaping death. And since this disposition, which forever prevents him from wishing this, arises from himself, he lays down his life not of necessity, but of free authority.

Boso. But those powers were not in all respects similar, the power to lie and the power to preserve his life. For, if he wished to lie, he would of course be able to; but, if he wished to avoid the other, he could no more do it than he could avoid being what he is. For he became man for this purpose, and it was on the faith of his coming death that he could receive birth from a virgin, as you said above.

Anselm. As you think that he could not lie, or that his death was necessary, because be could not avoid being what he was, so you can assert that he could not wish to avoid death, or that he wished to die of necessity, because he could not change the constitution of his being; for he did not become man in order that he should die, any more than for this purpose, that he should wish to die. Wherefore, as you ought not to say that he could not help wishing to die, or that it was of necessity that he wished to die, it is equally improper to say that he could not avoid death, or that he died of necessity.

Boso. Yes, since dying and wishing to die are included in the same mode of reasoning, both would seem to fall under a like necessity.

Anselm. Who freely wished to become man, that by the same unchanging desire he should suffer death, and that the virgin from whom that man should be born might be pure, through confidence in the certainty of this?

Boso. God, the Son of God.

Anselm. Was it not above shown, that no desire of God is at all constrained; but that it freely maintains itself in his own unchangeableness, as often as it is said that he does anything necessarily?

Boso. It has been clearly shown. But we see, on the other hand, that what God unchangeably wishes cannot avoid being so, but takes place of necessity. Wherefore, if God wished that man to die, he could but die.

Anselm. Because the Son of God took the nature of man with this desire, viz., that he should suffer death, you prove it necessary that this man should not be able to avoid death.

Boso. So I perceive.

Anselm. Has it not in like manner appeared from the things which we have spoken that the Son of God and the man whose person he took were so united that the same being should be both God and man, the Son of God and the son of the virgin?

Boso. It is so.

Anselm. Therefore the same man could possibly both die and avoid death.

Boso. I cannot deny it.

Anselm. Since, then, the will of God does nothing by any necessity, but of his own power, and the will of that man was the same as the will of God, he died not necessarily, but only of his own power.

Boso. To your arguments I cannot object; for neither your propositions nor your inferences can I invalidate in the least. But yet this thing which I have mentioned always recurs to my mind: that, if he wished to avoid death, he could no more do it than he could escape existence. For it must have been fixed that he was to die, for had it not been true that he was about to die, faith in his coming death would not have existed, by which the virgin who gave him birth and many others also were cleansed from their sin. Wherefore, if he could avoid death, he could make untrue what was true.

Anselm. Why was it true, before he died, that he was certainly to die?

Boso. Because this was his free and unchangeable desire.

Anselm. If, then, as you say, he could not avoid death because he was certainly to die, and was on this account certainly to die because it was his free and unchangeable desire, it is clear that his inability to avoid death is nothing else but his fixed choice to die.

Boso. This is so; but whatever be the reason, it still remains certain that he could not avoid death, but that it was a necessary thing for him to die.

Anselm. You make a great ado about nothing, or, as the saying is, you stumble at a straw.

Boso. Are you not forgetting my reply to the excuses you made at the beginning of our discussion, viz., that you should explain the subject, not as to learned men, but to me and my fellow inquirers? Suffer me, then, to question you as my slowness and dullness require, so that, as you have begun thus far, you may go on to settle all our childish doubts.

CHAPTER XVIII (A)[1]

How, with God there is neither necessity nor impossibility, and what is a coercive necessity, and what one that is not so.

Anselm. We have already said that it is improper to affirm of God that he does anything, or that he cannot do it, of necessity. For all necessity and impossibility is under his control. But his choice is subject to no necessity nor impossibility. For nothing is necessary or impossible save as He wishes it. Nay, the very choosing or refusing anything as a necessity or an impossibility is contrary to truth. Since, then, he does what he chooses and nothing else, as no necessity or impossibility exists before his choice or refusal, so neither do they interfere with his acting or not acting, though it be true that his choice and action are immutable. And as, when God does a thing, since it has been done it cannot be undone, but must remain an actual fact; still, we are not correct in saying that it is impossible for God to

---

1 This and the succeeding chapter are numbered differently in the different editions of Anselm's texts.

prevent a past action from being what it is. For there is no necessity or impossibility in the case whatever but the simple will of God, which chooses that truth should be eternally the same, for he himself is truth. Also, if he has a fixed determination to do anything, though his design must be destined to an accomplishment before it comes to pass, yet there is no coercion as far as he is concerned, either to do it or not to do it, for his will is the sole agent in the case. For when we say that God cannot do a thing, we do not deny his power; on the contrary, we imply that he has invincible authority and strength. For we mean simply this, that nothing can compel God to do the thing which is said to be impossible for him. We often use an expression of this kind, that a thing can be when the power is not in itself, but in something else; and that it cannot be when the weakness does not pertain to the thing itself, but to something else. Thus we say "Such a man can be bound," instead of saying, "Somebody can bind him," and, "He cannot be bound," instead of, "Nobody can bind him." For to be able to be overcome is not power but weakness, and not to be able to be overcome is not weakness but power. Nor do we say that God does anything by necessity, because there is any such thing pertaining to him, but because it exists in something else, precisely as I said with regard to the affirmation that he cannot do anything. For necessity is always either compulsion or restraint; and these two kinds of necessity operate variously by turn, so that the same thing is both necessary and impossible. For whatever is obliged to exist is also prevented from non-existence; and that which is compelled not to exist is prevented from existence. So that whatever exists from necessity cannot avoid existence, and it is impossible for a thing to exist which is under a necessity of nonexistence, and *vice versa*. But when we say with regard to God, that anything is necessary or not necessary, we do not mean that, as far as he is concerned, there is any necessity either coercive or prohibitory, but we mean that there is a necessity in everything else, restraining or driving them in a particular way. Whereas we say the very opposite of God. For, when we affirm that it is necessary for God to utter truth, and never to lie, we only mean that such is his unwavering disposition to maintain the truth that of necessity nothing can avail to make him deviate from the truth, or utter a lie. When, then, we say that that man (who, by the union of persons, is also God, the Son of God) could not avoid death, or the choice of death, after he was born of the virgin, we do not imply that there was in him any weakness with regard to preserving or choosing to preserve his life, but we refer to the unchangeableness of his purpose, by which he freely became man for this design, viz., that by persevering in his wish he should suffer death. And this desire nothing could shake. For it would be rather weakness than power if he could wish to lie, or deceive, or change his disposition, when before he had chosen that it should remain unchanged. And, as I said before, when one has freely determined to do some good action, and afterwards goes on to complete it, though, if unwilling to pay his vow, he could be compelled to do so, yet we must not say that he does it of necessity, but with the same freedom with which he made the resolution. For we ought not to say that anything is done, or not done, by necessity or weakness, when free choice is the only agent in the case. And, if this is so with regard to man, much less can we speak of necessity or weakness in reference to God; for he does nothing except according to his choice, and his will no force can drive or restrain. For this end was accomplished by the united natures of Christ, viz., that the Divine nature should perform that part of the work needful for man's restoration which the human nature could not do; and that in the human should be manifested what was inappropriate to the Divine. Finally, the virgin herself, who was made pure by faith in him, so that he might be born of her, even she, I say, never believed that he was to die, save of his own choice. For she knew the words of the prophet, who said of him: "He was offered of his own will." Therefore, since her faith was well founded, it must necessarily turn out as she believed. And, if it perplexes you to have me say that it is necessary, remember that the reality of the virgin's faith was not the cause of his dying by his own free will; but, because this was destined to take place, therefore her faith was real. If, then, it be said that it was necessary for him to die of his single choice, because the antecedent faith and prophecy were true, this is no more than saying that it must be because it was to be. But such a necessity as this does not compel a thing to be, but only implies a necessity of its existence. There is an antecedent necessity which is the cause of a thing, and there is also a subsequent necessity arising from the thing itself. Thus, when the heavens are said to revolve, it is an antecedent and efficient necessity, for they must revolve. But when I say that you speak of necessity, because you are speaking, this is nothing but a subsequent and inoperative necessity. For I only mean that it is impossible for you to speak and not to speak at the same time, and not that some one compels you to speak. For the force of its own nature makes the heaven revolve; but no necessity obliges you to speak. But wherever there is an antecedent necessity, there is also a subsequent one; but not vice versa. For we can say that the heaven revolves of necessity, because it revolves; but it is not likewise true that, because you speak, you do it of necessity. This subsequent necessity pertains to everything, so that we say: Whatever has been, necessarily has been. Whatever is, must be. Whatever is to be, of necessity will be. This is that necessity which Aristotle treats of ("*de propositionibus singularibus et futuris*"), and which seems to destroy any alternative and to ascribe a necessity to all things. By this subsequent and imperative necessity, was it necessary (since the belief and prophecy concerning Christ were true, that he would die of his own free will), that it should be so. For this he became man; for this he did and suffered all things undertaken by him; for this he chose as he did. For therefore were they necessary, because they were to be, and they were to be because they were, and they were because they were; and, if you wish to know the real necessity of all things which he did and suffered, know that they were of necessity, because he wished them to be. But no necessity preceded his will. Wherefore if they were not save by his will, then, had he not willed they would not have existed. So then, no one took his life from him, but he laid it down of himself and took it again; for he had power to lay it down and to take it again, as he himself said.

Boso. You have satisfied me that it cannot be proved that he was subjected to death by any necessity; and I cannot regret my importunity in urging you to make this explanation.

Anselm. I think we have shown with sufficient clearness how it was that God took a man without sin from a sinful substance; but I would on no account deny that there is no other explanation than this which we have given, for God can certainly do what human reason cannot grasp. But since this appears adequate, and since in search of other arguments we should involve ourselves in such questions as that of original sin, and how it was transmitted by our first parents to all mankind, except this man of whom we are speaking; and since, also, we should be drawn into various other questions, each demanding its own separate consideration; let us be satisfied with this account of the matter, and go on to complete our intended work.

Boso. As you choose; but with this condition that, by the help of God, you will sometime give this other explanation, which you owe me, as it were, but which now you avoid discussing.

Anselm. Inasmuch as I entertain this desire myself, I will not refuse you; but because of the uncertainty of future events, I dare not promise you, but commend it to the will of God. But say now, what remains to be unravelled with regard to the question which you proposed in the first place, and which involves many others with it?

Boso. The substance of the inquiry was this, why God became man, for the purpose of saving men by his death, when he could have done it in some other way. And you, by numerous and positive reasons, have shown that the restoring of mankind ought not to take place, and could not, without man paid the debt which he owed God for his sin. And this debt was so great that, while none but man must solve the debt, none but God was able to do it; so that he who does it must be both God and man. And hence arises a necessity that God should take man into unity with his own person; so that he who in his own nature was bound to pay the debt, but could not, might be able to do it in the person of God. In fine, you have shown that that man, who was also God, must be formed from the virgin, and from the person of the Son of God, and that he could be taken without sin, though from a sinful substance. Moreover, you have clearly shown the life of this man to have been so excellent and so glorious as to make ample satisfaction for the sins of the whole world, and even infinitely more. It now, therefore, remains to be shown how that payment is made to God for the sins of men.

Chapter XVIII (B)

How Christ's life is paid to God for the sins of men, and in what sense Christ ought, and in what sense he ought not, or was not bound, to suffer.

Anselm. If he allowed himself to be slain for the sake of justice, he did not give his life for the honor of God?

Boso. It should seem so, but I cannot understand, although I do not doubt it, how he could do this reasonably. If I saw how he could be perfectly holy, and yet forever preserve his life, I would acknowledge that he freely gave, for the honor of God, such a gift as surpasses all things else but God himself, and is able to atone for all the sins of men.

Anselm. Do you not perceive that when he bore with gentle patience the insults put upon him, violence and even crucifixion among thieves that he might maintain strict holiness; by this he set men an example that they should never turn aside from the holiness due to God on account of personal sacrifice? But how could he have done this, had he, as he might have done, avoided the death brought upon him for such a reason?

Boso. But surely there was no need of this, for many persons before his coming, and John the Baptist after his coming but before his death, had sufficiently enforced this example by nobly dying for the sake of the truth.

Anselm. No man except this one ever gave to God what he was not obliged to lose, or paid a debt he did not owe. But he freely offered to the Father what there was no need of his ever losing, and paid for sinners what he owed not for himself. Therefore he set a much nobler example, that each one should not hesitate to give to God, for himself, what he must at any rate lose before long, since it was the voice of reason; for he, when not in want of anything for himself and not compelled by others, who deserved nothing of him but punishment, gave so precious a life, even the life of so illustrious a personage, with such willingness.

Boso. You very nearly meet my wishes; but suffer me to make one inquiry, which you may think foolish, but which, nevertheless, I find no easy thing to answer. You say that when he died he gave what he did not owe. But no one will deny that it was better for him, or that so doing he pleased God more than if he had not done it. Nor will any one say that he was not bound to do what was best to be done, and what he knew would be more pleasing to God. How then can we affirm that he did not owe God the thing which he did, that is, the thing which he knew to be best and most pleasing to God, and especially since every creature owes God all that he is and all that he knows and all that he is capable of?

Anselm. Though the creature has nothing of himself, yet when God grants him the liberty of doing or not doing a thing, he leaves the alternative with him, so that, though one is better than the other, yet neither is positively demanded. And, whichever he does, it may be said that he ought to do it; and if he takes the better choice, he deserves a reward; because he renders freely what is his own. For, though celibacy be better than marriage, yet neither is absolutely enjoined upon man; so that both he who chooses marriage and he who prefers celibacy, may be said to do as they ought. For no one says that either celibacy or marriage ought not to be chosen; but we say that what a man esteems best before taking action upon any of these things, this he ought to do. And if a man preserves his celibacy as a free gift offered to God, he looks for a reward. When you say that the creature owes God what he knows to be the better choice, and what he is able to do, if you mean that he owes it as a debt, without implying any command on the part of God, it is not always true. Thus, as I have already said, a man is not bound to celibacy as a debt, but ought to marry if he prefers it. And if you are unable to understand the use of this word "*debere*," when no debt is implied, let me inform you that we use the word "*debere*" precisely as we sometimes do the words "*posse*," and "*non posse*," and also "*necessitas*," when the ability, etc., is not in the things themselves, but in something else. When, for instance, we say that the poor ought to receive alms from the rich, we mean that the rich ought to bestow alms upon the poor. For this is a debt not owed by the poor but by the rich. We also say that God ought to be exalted over all, not because there is any obligation resting upon him, but because all things ought to be subject to him. And he wishes that all creatures should be what they ought; for what God wishes to be ought to be. And, in like manner, when any creature wishes to do a thing that is left entirely at his own disposal, we say that he ought to do it, for what he wishes to be ought to be.

So our Lord Jesus, when he wished, as we have said, to suffer death, ought to have done precisely what he did; because he ought to be what he wished, and was not bound to do anything as a debt. As he is both God and man, in connection with his human nature, which made him a man, he must also have received from the Divine nature that control over himself which freed him from all obligation, except to do as he chose. In like manner, as one person of the Trinity, he must have had whatever he possessed of his own right, so as to be complete in himself, and could not have been under obligations to another, nor have need of giving anything in order to be repaid himself.

Boso. Now I see clearly that he did not give himself up to die for the honor of God, as a debt; for this my own reason proves, and yet he ought to have done what he did.

Anselm. That honor certainly belongs to the whole Trinity; and, since he is very God, the Son of God, he offered himself for his own honor, as well as for that of the Father and the Holy Spirit; that is, he gave his humanity to his divinity, which is one person of the Triune God. But, though we express our idea more definitely by clinging to the precise truth, yet we may say, according to our custom, that the Son freely gave himself to the Father. For thus we plainly affirm that in speaking of one person we understand the whole Deity, to whom as man he offered himself. And, by the names of Father and Son, a wondrous depth of devotion is excited in the hearts of the hearers, when it is said that the Son supplicates the Father on our behalf.

Boso. This I readily acknowledge.

Chapter XIX

How human salvation follows upon his death.

Anselm. Let us now observe, if we can, how the salvation of men rests on this.

Boso. This is the very wish of my heart. For, although I think I understand you, yet I wish to get from you the close chain of argument.

Anselm. There is no need of explaining how precious was the gift which the Son freely gave.

Boso. That is clear enough already.

Anselm. But you surely will not think that he deserves no reward, who freely gave so great a gift to God.

Boso. I see that it is necessary for the Father to reward the Son; else he is either unjust in not wishing to do it, or weak in not being able to do it; but neither of these things can be attributed to God.

Anselm. He who rewards another either gives him something which he does not have, or else remits some rightful claim upon him. But anterior to the great offering of the Son, all things belonging to the Father were his, nor did he ever owe anything which could be forgiven him. How then can a reward be bestowed on one who needs nothing, and to whom no gift or release can be made?

Boso. I see on the one hand a necessity for a reward, and on the other it appears impossible; for God must necessarily render payment for what he owes, and yet there is no one to receive it.

Anselm. But if a reward so large and so deserved is not given to him or any one else, then it will almost appear as if the Son had done this great work in vain.

Boso. Such a supposition is impious.

Anselm. The reward then must be bestowed upon some one else, for it cannot be upon him.

Boso. This is necessarily so.

Anselm. Had the Son wished to give some one else what was due to him, could the Father rightfully prevent it, or refuse to give it to the other person?

Boso. No! but I think it would be both just and necessary that the gift should be given by the Father to whomsoever the Son wished; because the Son should be allowed to give away what is his own, and the Father cannot bestow it at all except upon some other person.

Anselm. Upon whom would he more properly bestow the reward accruing from his death, than upon those for whose salvation, as right reason teaches, he became man; and for whose sake, as we have already said, he left an example of suffering death to preserve holiness? For surely in vain will men imitate him, if they be not also partakers of his reward. Or whom could he more justly make heirs of the inheritance, which he does not need, and of the superfluity of his possessions, than his parents and brethren? What more proper than that, when he beholds so many of them weighed down by so heavy a debt, and wasting through poverty, in the depth of their miseries, he should remit the debt incurred by their sins, and give them what their transgressions had forfeited?

Boso. The universe can hear of nothing more reasonable, more sweet, more desirable. And I receive such confidence from this that I cannot describe the joy with which my heart exults. For it seems to me that God can reject none who come to him in his name.

Anselm. Certainly not, if he come aright. And the Scriptures, which rest on solid truth as on a firm foundation, and which, by the help of God, we have somewhat examined, -- the Scriptures, I say, show us how to approach in order to share such favor, and how we ought to live under it.

Boso. And whatever is built on this foundation is founded on an immovable rock.

Anselm. I think I have nearly enough answered your inquiry, though I might do it still more fully, and there are doubtless many reasons which are beyond me and which mortal ken does not reach. It is also plain that God had no need of doing the thing spoken of, but eternal truth demanded it. For though God is said to have done what that man did, on account of the personal union made; yet God was in no need of descending from heaven to conquer the devil, nor of contending against him in holiness to free mankind. But God demanded that man should conquer the devil, so that he who had offended by sin should atone by holiness. As God owed nothing to the devil but punishment, so man must only make amends by conquering the devil as man had already been conquered by him. But whatever was demanded of man, he owed to God and not to the devil.

Chapter XX

How great and how just is God's compassion.

Now we have found the compassion of God which appeared lost to you when we were considering God's holiness and man's sin; we have found it, I say, so great and so consistent with his holiness, as to be incomparably above anything that can be conceived. For what compassion can excel these words of the Father, addressed to the sinner doomed to eternal torments and having no way of escape: "Take my only begotten Son and make him an offering for yourself;" or these words of the Son: "Take me, and ransom your souls." For these are the voices they utter, when inviting and leading us to faith in the Gospel. Or can anything be more just than for him to remit all debt since he has earned a reward greater than all debt, if given with the love which he deserves.

Chapter XXI

How it is impossible for the devil to be reconciled.

If you carefully consider the scheme of human salvation, you will perceive the reconciliation of the devil, of which you made inquiry, to be impossible. For, as man could not be reconciled but by the death of the God-man, by whose holiness the loss occasioned by man's sin should be made up; so fallen angels cannot be saved but by the death of a God-angel who by his holiness may repair the evil occasioned by the sins of his companions. And as man must not be restored by a man of a different race, though of the same nature, so no angel ought to be saved by any other angel, though all were of the same nature, for they are not like men, all of the same race. For all angels were not sprung from one, as all men were. And there is another objection to their restoration, viz, that, as they fell with none to plot their fall, so they must rise with none to aid them; but this is impossible. But otherwise they cannot be restored to their original dignity. For, had they not sinned, they would have been confirmed in virtue without any foreign aid, simply by the power given to them from the first. And, therefore, if any one thinks that the redemption of our Lord ought to be extended even to the fallen angels, he is convinced by reason, for by reason he has been deceived. And I do not say this as if to deny that the virtue of his death far exceeds all the sins of men and angels, but because infallible reason rejects the reconciliation of the fallen angels.

Chapter XXII

How the truth of the Old and New Testament is shown in the things which have been said.

Boso. All things which you have said seem to me reasonable and incontrovertible. And by the solution of the single question proposed do I see the truth of all that is contained in the Old and New Testament. For, in proving that God became man by necessity, leaving out what was taken from the Bible, viz., the remarks on the persons of the Trinity, and on Adam, you convince both Jews and Pagans by the mere force of reason. And the God-man himself originates the New Testament and approves the Old. And, as we must acknowledge him to be true, so no one can dissent from anything contained in these books.

Anselm. If we have said anything that needs correction, I am willing to make the correction if it be a reasonable one. But, if the conclusions which we have arrived at by reason seem confirmed by the testimony of the truth, then ought we to attribute it, not to ourselves, but to God, who is blessed forever.

Amen.